ART & DESIGN

ACADEMY GROUP LTD
42 LEINSTER GARDENS, LONDON W2 3AN
TEL: 0171-402 2141 FAX: 0171-723 9540

EDITOR: Nicola Kearton
ASSISTANT EDITOR: Ramona Khambatta
ART EDITOR: Andrea Bettella
CHIEF DESIGNER: Mario Bettella
DESIGNERS: James Powley, Alex Young

SUBSCRIPTION OFFICES:
UK: ACADEMY GROUP LTD
42 LEINSTER GARDENS
LONDON W2 3AN
TEL: 0171 402 2141 FAX: 0171723 9540

USA AND CANADA: VCH PUBLISHERS, INC
333 SEVENTH AVENUE, FIFTH FLOOR,
NEW YORK, NY 10001, USA
TEL: (212) 629 6200 FAX: (212) 629 8140

ALL OTHER COUNTRIES:
VCH VERLAGSGESELLSCHAFT MBH
BOSCHSTRASSE 12, POSTFACH 101161
69451 WEINHEIM
FEDERAL REPUBLIC OF GERMANY
TEL: 06201 606 148 FAX: 06201 606 184

© 1996 *Academy Group Ltd*. All rights reserved. No part of this publication may be reproduced or transmitted in any form or by any means, electronic or mechanical, including photocopying, recording or any information storage or retrieval system without permission in writing from the Publishers. Neither the Editor nor the Academy Group hold themselves responsible for the opinions expressed by writers of articles or letters in this magazine. The Editor will give careful consideration to unsolicited articles, photographs and drawings; please enclose a stamped addressed envelope for their return (if required). Payment for material appearing in *A&D* is not normally made except by prior arrangement. All reasonable care will be taken of material in the possession of *A&D* and agents and printers, but they regret that they cannot be held responsible for any loss or damage.
Subscription rates for 1996 (incl p&p): *Annual subscription price*: UK only £65.00, World DM 195 for regular subscribers. *Student rate*: UK only £50.00, World DM 156 incl postage and handling charges. *Individual issues*: £17.95/DM 42.50 (plus £2.30/DM 5 for p&p, per issue ordered).
For the USA and Canada: *Art & Design* is published six times per year (Jan/Feb; Mar/Apr; May/Jun; Jul/Aug; Sept/Oct; and Nov/Dec) by Academy Group Ltd, 42 Leinster Gardens, London W2 3AN, England and distributed by VCH Publishers New York Inc., Suite 907, 220 East 23rd Street, New York, NY 10010-4606, USA. Annual subscription price; US $135.00 including postage and handling charges; special student rates available at $105.00, single issue $28.95. Second-class postage paid at New York, NY. **POSTMASTER**: Send address changes to Art & Design, c/o VCH New York Inc., Suite 907, 220 East 23rd Street, New York, NY 10010-4606, USA

Printed in Italy. All prices are subject to change without notice. [ISSN: 0267-3991]
The full text of *Art & Design* is also available in the electronic versions of the Art Index.

CONTENTS

Carrie Mae Weems, Untitled, 1990, edition of five, silver print, 71.6x 71.6xcm

Carrie Walter Stettheimer's doll's house, kitchen, c 1916-35

Linda Hudson, Moving In (detail), Home Show 2, 1996

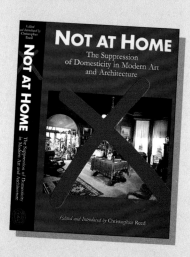

HOMES AND GARDENS Documenting the Invisible: Images of Kosovo by Melanie Friend, Camerawork Limited, London, 1996, £5.00

A home symbolises security, protection and privacy from the outside world; a home is commonly regarded as a sanctuary. That is, of course, a home where this symbolism is valued. In nations or regions torn apart by warring factions, however, nothing is sacred, and when one hears of innocent lives being violated within their own homes, the tragedy of the situation is heightened.

Newspaper editors lean towards publishing violent images, the theory behind this being the more blood and carnage, the greater the public interest in the paper. This may well be the case, but it has come to the point where the general public displays an almost blasé reaction to such images. Each individual incident is tragic but not as disturbing as what Melanie Friend has opened our eyes to; a report of brutal violence in private homes as a method of 'slow motion ethnic cleansing' in which the images reflect peaceful homeliness, not horrific evidence of brutal suffering.

Historically, 'ethnic cleansing' is sadly not an anomaly. Over the past 50 years peaceful nations have striven to eradicate such bigoted violence but in practice this has not been successful, as Melanie Friend, a photo-journalist, has shown us in her joint exhibition (June-July 1996) and publication, *Homes and Gardens*, which focuses on Kosovo, an area populated in large by Albanians in SW Serbia, which the Serbs are intent on 'cleansing'. Friend has visited Kosovo three times in a professional capacity and was determined to make the world aware of the plight of the people in this little known area of Eastern Europe. Her attempts to photograph and record the violence were thwarted at every opportunity, which forced her to think of an alternative method to relay her message. She chose to represent the horrors 'invisibly' – instead of photographing the tortured victims, Friend photographed the immaculate rooms and gardens of the homes which had witnessed such 'cleansing', with both the exhibition and booklet including accompanying accounts by the victims.

Each room, each garden, was meticulously cleaned and tidied after each Serbian police attack, the pride of the locals standing tall against such flagrant acts of unlawfulness. This is what Melanie Friend has photographed – these homes which look so lived in, so family-oriented, so welcoming and safe. The photographs alone are witness to the normal lives we all know and feel comfortable with; it is when the victims' accounts are heard or read, does the illusion become glaringly harsh.

Friend's message is strong and has the desired effect; it is a visual testimony which leaves one fearful, haunted by the images and words which tear down our reassuring sense of security.

The booklet closes with two pieces which relate closely to the theme of the publication. Firstly, there are extracts from a stark interview conducted with Arta Dedaj and Barbara Hunt, the former a graduate of the University of Prishtina, who has lived and worked in London since 1991 and has applied for asylum. A brief chronology of events is preceded by an Afterword on Shock Theory by David Bates, a parallel commentary on our social world and the problems of representation in it.

Ramona Khambatta

NOT AT HOME The Suppression of Domesticity in Modern Art and Architecture edited by Christopher Reed, Thames and Hudson, London, 1996, HB, £19.95, 336pp

The position of domesticity in the development of modern art and architecture has mostly been defined by its lack. It is not just the image of domesticity itself that has caused this negative view, but more its associations. These have revolved around divisions of feminine/masculine, high/low, professional/amateur. This associative status has allowed it to be removed from much art historical and architectural debate, when it does appear its treatment is often antagonistic.

Theories of modernism have tended to impose a strict value system that establishes a hierarchy that cannot easily be broken. The linking of the domestic with the decorative and the feminine have been elements that have placed it outside modernist consideration. The figure of Baudelaire dominates much of the early writings on modernity and modernism. The image of the artist as 'flaneur' who documents experience of the city was part of the change to the acceptability of a wider subject matter. The salon hierarchy of value with history painting at its head was overturned, yet the domestic was still to play a lowly role. The work of Berthe Morisot and Mary Cassatt gives more an indication of the gendering of space than any promotion of domesticity purely for its own sake.

Not at Home provides a wide-ranging survey of many of the issues that have seen the suppression of domesticity in modern art and architecture. The 17 essays collected in the book cut across late 19th and 20th-century Europe and America. What at first seems like a document of the complete absence of domesticity slowly comes to be seen as a suppression, but one with a traceable history. The essays construct a variety of modernisms against which to play the image of the domestic, which has been used to reinforce strict divisions of masculine and feminine, but also as a way of rebelling against unchallenged notions of normality. This is, perhaps, where the book is at its most successful.

In Lisa Tiersten's essay the interiors of *fin-de-siècle* Paris are shown as arenas of complex relations. The 'housewife-as-artist' figure is seen as creating a paradigm of modernism that is both feminine and domestic, and therefore a challenge to the canonical view. In 'Master Bedrooms, Master Narratives', Kenneth Silver looks at the use of homosexuality to subvert the domestic setting. In the case of Francis Bacon this was achieved by appropriating Muybridge's wrestling figures into a domestic interior and sexualising the activity. With David Hockney it is the very 'ordinariness' of the image that becomes a challenge in itself.

In the Introduction, Christopher Reed acknowledges the work of Le Corbusier and Clement

Greenberg, both of whose writings have proved influential. It is precisely the type of modernist orthodoxies set up by Le Corbusier and Greenberg that *Not at Home* sets out to challenge. Le Corbusier's oft quoted maxim of the home as 'a machine for living in' is the antithesis of most ideas of domesticity. In a similar uncompromising outlook for art, Greenberg's concentration on the 'ineluctable flatness' of the picture surface sets up a series of priorities that left issues of domesticity marginalised.

In Lisa Wainwright's examination of the use of fabric in the work of Robert Rauschenberg, its meaning works at a variety of levels. It was a reaction against the masculine, and indeed macho concerns of Abstract Expressionism, a disturbing of the boundaries between high and low, as well as an archiving of Rauschenberg's own past and present life. The fabric's association with femininity and its craft status were what made this work particularly effective.

As Reed warns in the Introduction, 'the repressed always returns', giving an indication of the book's intention and the general pattern it maps out of suppression, subversion followed by re-integration.

It has been postmodernism that has provided a more important place for domesticity and in its turn part of the challenge to modernism. Reed and Haar note that Pop art and feminism are able to use domesticity as 'a central element in their defiance of modernism, though with very different motives and effects'. This sort of defiance can be seen most clearly in a project such as 'Womanhouse'. This project, created by 23 women from the Feminist Art Program in California, takes the very site of domesticity, the home itself, and turns it into an art object. An abandoned mansion becomes a walk-in installation on the conditions and conditioning of women's lives.

The image of domesticity has been prone to the creation of stereotypes of a particularly shallow kind. With *Not at Home*, an exploration is possible of some of the contested sites of domesticity in modernism in a more rational and much needed way.

Steven Gartside

THE DINNER PARTY by Judy Chicago, Penguin Books, New York, 1996, PB, 234pp, £15.00
First exhibited almost 20 years ago, Judy Chicago's *The Dinner Party* installation attempted a novel representation of women using non-traditional media. At the same time, it employed the highly traditional techniques of plate-making and embroidery – both practices associated with women and domesticity – to illustrate the history of women in Western civilisation in symbolic form. *The Dinner Party* forged a new visual language with its imagery that incorporated vulval motifs; but this very imagery provoked a barrage of attack from the New York art world: the work was seen by some critics to be anything from grotesquely 'kitsch' to simply 'vaginas on plates'. Several years later in 1990, after a decision to donate the work to a prospective arts centre at the University of the District of Columbia, *The Dinner Party* was castigated as 'pornographic' in the US Congress: again, 'three-dimensional ceramic art of 39 women's vaginal areas, their genitalia, served up on plates'.

This book shows more than just the plates, however, and presents the work in its context, both visually and historically. It illustrates each aspect of the 39-place settings: the painted plates (whose imagery, Chicago reminds us, is rooted in vulval and butterfly forms, transmuted and layered) and their elaborately needle-worked or textile-crafted runners which themselves provide a context for each plate by comprising motifs and styles of the period in which the women lived, symbolising the conditions of their respective environments; the Millennium Triangles (the three corners of the triangular table) are also featured. The life of the work is documented in Chicago's text, in which she relates the background to the project, the women with whom she collaborated in the making of the work as well as the research of the female figures; the exhibiting (and the cancelled exhibitions), reception and controversy of the work; and the projects, events and grass-roots support movement it generated which ensured its exhibition in alternative spaces.

The Dinner Party book is published on the occasion of *The Dinner Party*'s commemorative exhibition at the UCLA Armand Hammer Museum in Los Angeles. The book can also be seen as a reference work in its own right, not simply of the work's own progression through time but, more importantly, of the women featured and their significance in their own times. As symbols they can be experienced visually through *The Dinner Party* installation, and the book can be read as a textual elaboration of the visual piece. A paean to the women featured in the work – not only those seated at the table but the 999 individuals inscribed on the central part of the installation – the porcelain Heritage Floor (which has tended to be the least focused-upon part of the work due to its text-based presentation), the majority of the book charts in chronological sections all the women in the work and offers a biographical entry of each. As such it is a highly informative dictionary of 1,038 women through the ages; a narrative as well as visual tour of the work that offers an insight into women's heritage.

Vivian Constantinopoulos

RACHEL WHITEREAD: HOUSE edited by James Lingwood, Phaidon Press, London, 1995, £17.99, 144pp
The book survives as a moving testimony in words and pictures to Rachel Whiteread's cast of a Victorian terraced house in the East End of London. Commissioned by Artangel and completed in the autumn of 1993, the making of *House* caused extreme and complex reactions in many areas of public life from the streets of Bow to the House of Commons. This culminated in Whiteread being awarded the 1993 Turner Prize, but *House*'s brief moment of glory ended in January 1994 when by order of Bow Neighbourhood Council it was demolished.

The sculpture, a concrete 'funereal' cast of the existing structure taken from the inside, presented a vision of private domestic space solidified and frozen in time. It was never supposed to be permanent, unlike Whiteread's other pieces, for instance *Ghost*, the cast of the cramped internal space of a bed-sit in Archway. Yet, ironically it was the battle to prevent or hasten its destruction which propelled it into the news.

The book sets out to explore quite what it was about *House* that touched so many nerve endings and why it has been seen as one of the greatest public sculptures made by an English artist this century.

House was itself a memorial to the working-class terraced house bombed in the Blitz, pulled down by post-war developers, or in the case of 193 Grove Road, planned to be demolished to make way for a green corridor of open spaces leading from Victoria Park to the Isle of Dogs. It drew quiet attention to the shifting geography of the East End.

Was the presence of *House* an affront to the instinct for urban rationalisation and slum clearance, an instinct which was heightened in the speculative land developments of the 80s? Did it not fit the sunny view of East End history plotted by the Bow Heritage Trail? Or was it offensive in an area where so many were homeless or severely disadvantaged, a crude misplacement of funds? Had Whiteread, by silencing the house forever, mutilated the archetypal space of homelessness and produced a disturbing vision of a home which could never be re-entered, an identity never regained?

It was clear that, in the tradition of Carl Andre's bricks, the sculpture provided another mile stone in the long running British debate about contemporary art. It was also another spectacular illustration of the difficulty of placing sculpture in public places. The book draws up the battle lines clearly between goodies and baddies, introducing the colourful figures of Sydney Gale, the house's last occupant, or Councillor Flounders of Bow, almost another Brian Sewall, to contemporary art demonology. Including essays by Jon Bird, Doreen Massey, Ian Sinclair and Anthony Vidler, the book is a rare event in art publishing: an indepth view of one extraordinarily rich work of art and a leisured examination of the host of meanings it engendered.

Nicola Kearton

ART & DESIGN MONOGRAPHS are a series of publications concentrating on artists and designers of lasting interest and importance. Often designed in close collaboration with the artists, the Monographs explore the careers of the individuals represented in words, images and critical writing highlighting both the works themselves and the thought processes that lie behind them.

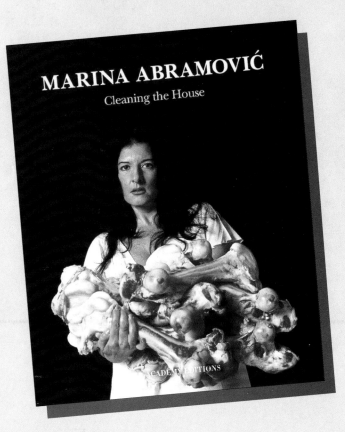

DAVID NASH
FORMS INTO TIME

With an Essay by Marina Warner

David Nash's career has been a profound exploration into the possibilities of form inherent in trees and timber. His sculptures combine a 20th-century sensibility with an ability to draw out the natural anatomy of different woods. Nash utilises traditional methods of woodsmanship gathered from all around the world evoking those agricultural skills increasingly lost in an industrial age. Within his pieces is a deeper echo of the importance of wood as shelter and fuel but also a potent symbol of both life and death in many cultures.

This book illustrates, in special pages designed by the artist, 14 themes that have run through his work for the last 30 years.

PB 1 85490 353 5
305 x 252 mm, 128 pages
Illustrated in colour throughout
1996

MARINA ABRAMOVIĆ
CLEANING THE HOUSE

For the past 25 years Marina Abramović's career has been a personal investigation of physical limits and mental potential through the performance medium. Her extensive travels and encounters with non-Western cultures as diverse as Tibet, the Aborigines of Australia and Sufism have led to the realisation that all these cultures pushed the body to the physical extreme in order to eliminate the fear of death, pain and the physical limitations of Western society. Abramović's works have increasingly centred on the mental and physical conditioning of the artist and the audience. *Cleaning the House* is an inner cleansing and self-organisation in the form of a deeply personal scrapbook of images of people, places texts designed in close collaboration with herself. There are very few books that consider the artist's motivations and emotions. This book shows the processes you never see. Reading it is an open experience where the reader can project and where some of these images might become their own.

PB 1 85490 399 3
305 x 252 mm, 120 pages
Over 100 colour illustrations
1995

Further information can be obtained from:
Academy Group Ltd, 42 Leinster Gardens, London W2 3AN, Tel:
0171 402 2141, Sales: 0171 402 3442 Fax: 0171 723 9540, or from
your local sales office.

National Book Network, 4720 Boston Way, Lanham, Maryland
20706, USA. Tel: (301) 459 3366
Fax: (301) 459 2118

VCH, Boschstrasse 12, Postfach 101161, 69451 Weinheim, Federal
Republic of Germany,
Tel: +49 6201 606 144 Fax: +49 6201 606 184

DAVID MACH

Essays by Paul Bonaventura and Tim Marlow

David Mach rose to prominence in the early 80s with his remarkable large scale sculpture projects, notably *Polaris*, the submarine made entirely from tyres exhibited at the South Bank Centre in London and his vast magazine sculptures such as *Fuel for the Fire* at the Riverside Studios in London. His unique sculpture is characterised by his use of components such as magazines, newspapers, matches and bottles, suggesting today's obsession with consumerism and the resulting levels of manufactured surplus and waste. He has exhibited in museums and galleries around the world, and also presents work in a variety of more open locations such as swimming baths, shopping malls, parks and gardens. Along with the striking visual quality of his sculpture this openness and accessibility has ensured Mach's popular status as well as his critical acclaim.

PB 1 85490 350 0
305 x 252 mm, 128 pages
Over 100 colour illustrations
1995

BRIAN CLARKE

Essay by Kenneth Powell

Starting with his first commissions in the early 70s, the artistic output of Brian Clarke has been extraordinary in its creative range, scope of projects and international appeal. His unique and thorough knowledge of drawings, paintings, gilding, mosaic, calligraphy, heraldry, tapestries and stained glass has led him to see various concepts of artistic mediums as essential and integrated parts of a unified architectural structure. His designs can be seen around the world in England, Germany, Spain, France, Japan, Saudi Arabia, Qatar and the United States. His design projects, frequently in stained glass, are in private homes; The New Synagogue in Darmstadt, Germany; Lake Sagami Country Club in Yamanishi, Japan; assorted shopping centres, corporations, and restaurants; Stansted Airport in England; stage sets for Paul McCartney's World Tour and for the tribute to Rudolf Nureyev; and the Stuttgart Museum of Natural History, Germany.

PB 1 85490 343 8
305 x 252 mm, 128 pages
Over 100 colour illustrations
1994

ARAKAWA & MADELINE GINS
ARCHITECTURE: SITES OF REVERSIBLE DESTINY

New York based artists Arakawa and Madeline Gins have collaborated on projects for over 30 years. This book is a unique and predominantly visual exploration into architecture, carrying philosophical argument into the realm of construction.

It asks what is the nature of perception in images of architectural constructions and how does the human being relate to the surrounding space? Arakawa and Gins have put together the first systematic study of the role the body and bodily movements play in the forming of the world. Through a series of computer generated images of intricacy the reader is taken on a visual journey.

Arguing that architecture is central to human life the book suggests a revolutionary reinventing of the planet and by extension the universe.

PB 1 85490 279 2
305 x 252 mm, 128 pages
Over 240 illustrations, mostly in colour
1995

NANCY WOLF
HIDDEN CITIES, HIDDEN LONGINGS

Karen A Franck

American architectural artist Nancy Wolf leads the reader through her life and art; from her earliest commentaries on architecture and society, to her most recent drawings which pose compelling alternatives to the anonymous modern cityscape. Wolf vividly portrays the sterility of Modernism, the superficiality of Post-Modernism, and the possibilities for change in Deconstructivism. She has integrated her pointed critiques of these architectural movements with her own experiences of alienation in an urban renewal area of Washington, DC, the devastation of New York in the 70s and 80s, and the intimacy of traditional communities in Africa and Asia. Wolf's message is clear: contemporary Western architecture and planning have lost sight of people; cities leave inhabitants disconnected from each other and from the places where they live and work.

A foreword by Peter Blake, an introduction by Karen A Franck and an informal dialogue between her and Nancy Wolf frame the spectacular images.

PB 1 85490 351 9
305 x 252 mm, 120 pages
Illustrated throughout
1996

STEPHEN WILLATS
BETWEEN BUILDINGS AND PEOPLE

This book explores the effect of the modernist built environment on people and how they express themselves creatively as individuals. Willats's work as an artist has been concerned for over 30 years with an exploration into social relations and the polemics of contemporary life in urban society. The book presents a series of interactive projects from Berlin, London and New York combining photographs and interviews with those who live within the 'new reality' of modernist architecture. The reader is introduced to a host of unforgettable characters who express alternative ways of maintaining their sense of identity and self-worth in an often hostile environment. It is a unique and humanistic view of architecture where people themselves are the starting point rather than buildings. As well as providing what could become an indispensable document about how people live, Willats's work is an important attempt to define the social role of art and to reflect the transience and fluidity of developments in culture.

PB 1 85490 436 1
252 x 190 mm, 144 pages
Over 100 b/w illustrations
1996

AUDIO ARTS
DISCOURSE AND PRACTICE IN CONTEMPORARY ART

William Furlong

The internationally renowned *Audio Arts*, the invention of two artists, William Furlong and Barry Barker, began in 1973 as the first and only art magazine to be published on audio cassette. A invaluable book for those seriously interested in contemporary art, this unique source of reference includes collaborations with leading international artists, interviews and archive recordings. Artists featured include Noam Chomsky, Wyndham Lewis, James Joyce, Marcel Duchamp, Howard Hodgkin, Andy Warhol, Joseph Beuys, Joseph Kosuth, Angela Bulloch, Rachel Whiteread, Susan Hiller, Laurie Anderson, Philip Glass, Hans Haacke, Nancy Spero and Jeff Koons.

PB 1 85490 363 2
279 x 217 mm, 144 pages
100 illustrations in colour and black and white
1994

F R A N K F U R T

Art in the Eye of the Beholder

Messe Frankfurt
Hall 1 – City Entrance

Opening Hours:
Sat. – Wed. 11 a. m. till 8 p. m.
Thurs. 11 a. m. till 6 p. m.

Information:
Phone: (0 69) 75 75 - 66 64
Fax: (0 69) 75 75 - 66 74
Internet:
http://www.messefrankfurt.de/art/

Action, Information, Discussion
The latest in contemporary art,
presented by galleries from all
over the world – together with the
flanking program, special shows
and unique Visitor School – make
encounters with art at Art Frankfurt
an inspiring experience.

ART Frankfurt
The fair that keeps to the subject of art
April 26 – May 1, 1997

Messe
Frankfurt

Art & Design

ART & THE HOME

ACADEMY EDITIONS • LONDON

Three Day Weekend is a project space located in Los Angeles. Shows are generally three days in length, taking place on holidays and their accompanying weekends. Three Day Weekend welcomes proposals and inquiries:

Attention: David Muller, 1422 Ridge Way, Los Angeles, CA 90026-4326, phone/fax: 213.481.0093

Some Three Day Weekend events will take place at this address. Others will be taking place at various sites in Los Angeles and who knows where else. Stay tuned for information as Three Day Weekend begins to move.

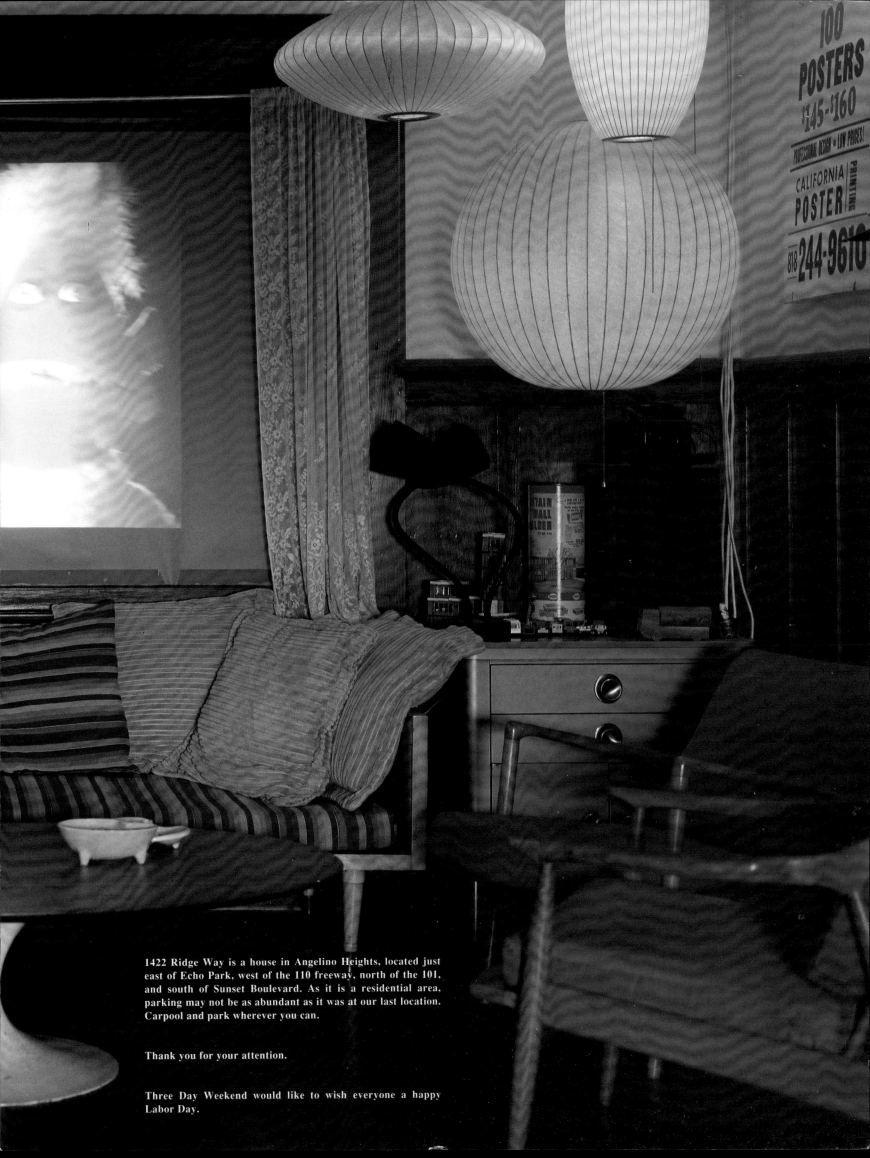

1422 Ridge Way is a house in Angelino Heights, located just east of Echo Park, west of the 110 freeway, north of the 101, and south of Sunset Boulevard. As it is a residential area, parking may not be as abundant as it was at our last location. Carpool and park wherever you can.

Thank you for your attention.

Three Day Weekend would like to wish everyone a happy Labor Day.

Acknowledgements

Art & Design would like to thank David A Greene for guest-editing this issue of *Art & Design* with its special American focus. We would also like to acknowledge the help of Jeffrey Kastner in the early phase of this project.

A version of Dave Hickey's 'A Home in the Neon' was originally published in *Art issues #35*, November/December 1994 (© The Foundation for Advanced Critical Studies). It will appear in *Air Guitar: Essays on Art and Democracy*, forthcoming from Art issues Press in 1997; a version of Karen Klabin's 'Safe as Houses' was originally published in *Detour* magazine, November 1995.

Unless otherwise stated, all images are courtesy of the artists: *Page 1* (above) Courtesy PPOW (New York), (centre) © Museum of the City of New York, Gift of Miss Ettie Stettheimer; *pp2-3* photo Miles Coolidge and Amy Russell; **A Home In The Neon** *pp6-9* p6 courtesy Rosamund Felsen Gallery (Santa Monica); **Rubén Ortiz-Torres** *p5, pp10-17* courtesy Jan Kesner Gallery (Los Angeles); **Luis Alfaro** *pp18-22* p18 courtesy Jan Kesner; **Sam Durant** *pp23-32* courtesy Blum & Poe (Santa Monica); **Mark Bennett** *pp33-37* photos Paula Goldman, courtesy Mark Moore Gallery (Santa Monica); **Uta Barth** *pp48-57* photos courtesy of ACME (Santa Monica) and Tanya Bonakdar Gallery (New York) with London Projects, UK; **By Any Means Necessary** *pp70-75* photos courtesy PPOW (New York); **The House That Carrie Built** *pp76-81* p76 courtesy Columbia University in the City of New York, Gift of the Estate of Ettie Stettheimer, 1967, pp79 (centre and below) © Museum of the City of New York, Gift of Miss Ettie Stettheimer, p80 (above, left) courtesy Jay Gorney Modern Art (New York), (above right) courtesy Davison Art Center, Wesleyan University, Gift of Mrs Rose Fried, 1964, (below left) © Museum of the City of New York (below, right) courtesy Janet Borden, Inc and the Whitney Museum of American Art (New York); **Jim Isermann** *pp82-89* courtesy of the artist, Feature Inc (New York) and Richard Telles Fine Art (Los Angeles), page design: PATCO.

Contributors' Biographies

David A Greene is a writer and critic living in New York City. He is Editor-at-Large of *Art issues* magazine; **David Muller** is an artist and the coordinator of Three Day Weekend, a project space in Los Angeles; **Dave Hickey** is a freelance writer and critic who lives in Las Vegas, Nevada; **Karen Klabin** is a Los Angeles writer specialising in public policy issues; **Luis Alfaro**, a Los Angeles native, is a playwright, performer, and the author of a spoken-word CD (*down town*, New Alliance/SST Records). His writing has been published in numerous anthologies, including *Sundays at Seven: Stories from a Different Light* (Alamo Square, 1996) and *The United States of Poetry* (Harry Abrams, 1996); **Rubén Ortiz-Torres** is an artist who lives in Los Angeles and Mexico City. He has exhibited at the Jan Kesner Gallery, Los Angeles, and is the director, with Jesse Lerner, of *Frontierland/Frontierlandia*, a film aired on PBS in 1995. His work was included in 'Distant Relations: A Dialogue between Chicano, Irish and Mexican artists', 1996 (the exhibition toured Camden Arts Centre, London, Ikon Gallery, Birmingham, the Irish Museum of Modern Art, Dublin, the Santa Monica Museum of Art and the Museo de Arte Carillo Gil, Mexico City); **Sam Durant** is represented by Blum & Poe Gallery in Santa Monica, CA. His work has been exhibited in Los Angeles, New York and London; **Mark Bennett**, an artist and postal carrier for the City of Beverly Hills, was born in Chattanooga, Tennessee. He has shown at Mark Moore Gallery, Santa Monica, and will be the subject of a one-person exhibition at the Corcoran Gallery of Art, Washington, DC, in 1997; **Miles Coolidge** was born in Montreal, Canada. He teaches at the California Institute of the Arts and the University of Southern California, and has shown at ACME in Santa Monica and Casey M Kaplan Gallery in New York; **Soo Jin Kim** is an artist and writer living in Los Angeles. She is a contributor to the catalogue for 'Hotel California', an exhibition at the Arlington Museum of Art in 1997, and is editor of *Things that Quicken the Heart* (CalArts Press, 1996); **Uta Barth** has had exhibitions at the Museum of Modern Art, New York, the Los Angeles County Museum of Art, and ACME, Santa Monica. She will be featured in a forthcoming exhibition at the Wexner Center, Ohio. A catalogue of her work was published by the Museum of Contemporary Art, Los Angeles, in 1995. Her first solo exhibition in Europe was held at London Projects, Frith Street, London, June 14-July 27 1996; **Michael Darling** is a critic based in Santa Barbara, California, whose writing has appeared in *Art issues*, *Frieze*, *Flash Art*, and *New Art Examiner*. He is at work on a book about the domestic furniture designs of American architect George Nelson; **Judy Fiskin** has had exhibitions at Curt Marcus Gallery, New York, the Patricia Faure Gallery, Santa Monica, and the Museum of Contemporary Art, Los Angeles. She recently received a Los Angeles Center for Photographic Studies Distinguished Career in Photography award; **Lucy Soutter** is a photographer, working towards a doctorate in the History of Art at Yale University; **Janine Mileaf** is a doctoral candidate in the History of Art at the University of Pennsylvania. She is completing her dissertation, 'From "Fountain" to Fetish: The Found Object in Dada and Surrealism, 1917-1936'; **Jim Isermann** was born in Kenosha, Wisconsin. He has had recent exhibitions at Richard Telles Fine Art, Los Angeles and Feature, New York, and will be included in 'How Will We Behave?' at Robert Prime Gallery, London.

FRONT COVER: Jim Isermann, Untitled, *1993, hand-pieced fabric wall hanging, 28.7x28.7cm (photo Peter Muscato)*
BACK COVER: Uta Barth, Ground #42, *1994, 4.4x4.1x0.9cm (photo Paula Goldman)*
INSIDE COVERS: Allan Wexler, Five Yardsaver Homes, *1996*
text (front) by Carrie Mae Weems, from Welcome Home, *1990; text (back) by Luis Alfaro, from* On A Street Corner

EDITOR: Nicola Kearton ASSISTANT EDITOR: Ramona Khambatta
ART EDITOR: Andrea Bettella CHIEF DESIGNER: Mario Bettella DESIGNERS: James Powley, Alex Young

First published in Great Britain in 1996 by *Art & Design* an imprint of
ACADEMY GROUP LTD, 42 LEINSTER GARDENS, LONDON W2 3AN
Member of the VCH Publishing Group
ISBN: 1 85490 235 0 (UK)

Art & Design Profile 51 is published as part of *Art & Design* Vol 11 11/12 1996
Art & Design Magazine is published six times a year and is available by subscription

Distributed to the trade in the United States of America by
NATIONAL BOOK NETWORK, INC, 4720 BOSTON WAY, LANHAM, MARYLAND 20706

Printed and bound in Italy

Contents

Rubén Ortiz-Torres, No Lo Hagas/Don't Do It, *East LA, 1991, 7.8x9.4cm*

ART & DESIGN PROFILE NO 51

ART & THE HOME

Guest-edited by David A Greene

Karen Carson, Spin, *1994, silkscreen, 81.3x71.1cm (photo Chris Warner)*

A HOME IN THE NEON

Dave Hickey

It's the strangest thing. I have lived in a lot of cities, some of them for substantial lengths of time, but I have never thought of any of them as home. I thought of them as 'where I'm living now'. Then, the other morning, I woke up and realised that Las Vegas has, indeed, become my home – that I routinely think of it as such. Somehow, in the few years that I have been living here and travelling out of here, this most un-homelike of cities has come to function for me as a kind of moral bottom-line – as a secular refuge and a source of comforts and reassurances that are unavailable elsewhere – as a home, in other words.

Yet, even as I write this, I realise that claiming Las Vegas as my home while practising 'art criticism' in the hyper-textualised, super-virtuous high culture of the 90s probably sounds a bit studied – a bit calculatedly exotic – as if I were trying to make a 'statement', or something. In truth, this condition of feeling at home in Las Vegas makes me wonder just how far back things really go, since, when I was a kid, whenever I heard about Las Vegas, it was always being discussed as a potential home by my Dad's jazz-musician buddies and their 'so-called wives' (as my Mom invariably referred to them).

This was back in the 50s when Las Vegas was rapidly becoming the only city in the American West where a professional musician might hold down a steady gig without living out of a suitcase. So, for my Dad's pals, Vegas shone out there in the desert like a grail, as a kind of outlaw town, like Butch Cassidy's Hole in the Wall or Fritz Lang's Rancho Notorious, where a tiring swing musician or a jive-talking bopster might find a refuge from the road, as well as from respectability. A player might work steadily in Vegas, and perhaps get a taste of Fat America, might rent a house in the suburbs, for instance – with a two-car garage and a yard, even – and still be able to play Charlie Parker in the kitchen at 4.00am and roll the occasional funny cigarette. In fact, the only time I was ever *in* Las Vegas as a child, we spent a hot afternoon in the dark kitchen of a pink-stucco bungalow doing approximately that.

While the sun glared outside, my Dad and his friend, Shelton, drank beer out of tall brown bottles and played Billie Holliday's *Gloomy Sunday* about a zillion times. The whole afternoon, Shelton kept marvelling at the ease with which he would pick up his axe later that evening, put it in the trunk of his Pontiac and drive down to his gig at the Desert Inn. He pantomimed this procedure two or three times, just to show us how easy it was, and that night we got to go with him to the Desert Inn, where there were a million lights, roulette wheels clicking and

guys in tuxedos who looked like Cornell Wilde. Outside the plate-glass windows we could see the turquoise swimming pool surrounded by rich, green grass, and there were white tablecloths on the tables in the lounge where we sat with other sophisticates and grooved to the music. I thought it was *great*, but my Dad got progressively grumpier as the evening wore on. He kept making remarks about Shelton's musicianship and I could tell that he was envious of his friend's steady gig.

So, having told you this, if I tell you that I now have a steady gig in Vegas, that I live two blocks from the Desert Inn and eat lunch there about once a week, you will understand my reservations about the possibility of our ever growing up – because, even though the days of steady gigs for sax maniacs are long gone, I still think of Vegas the way Shelton did: as a town where outsiders can still get work, three shifts a day, around the clock, seven days a week – and when not at work, may walk unmolested down the sidewalk in their choice of apparel. My brother calls Vegas a 'cowboy town', because 50-year-old heterosexual guys still room together here, and pairs of married couples share suburban homes, dividing up the bedrooms and filling the communal areas with beer cans and pizza boxes.

Most importantly for me, though, Vegas is a town that can serve as the heart's destination – a town where half the pick-up trucks stolen in Arizona, Utah, Montana and Wyoming are routinely recovered in casino parking lots – where 90 per cent of the population arises every morning absolutely delighted to have escaped Hometown, America, and the necessity of chatting with Mom over the back fence. This lightens the tone of social intercourse considerably. To cite an example, while I was having breakfast at the local IHOP the other morning, my waitress confided in me that, even though the International House of Pancakes was not the *greatest* organisation in the world, it had transferred her out of Ogden, Utah, and she was thankful for that. However, not so thankful, she said, that she planned to stay in 'food'. As soon as she got Lance in school, she was moving up to 'cocktail', where the tips were better.

She was looking forward to that, she said; and, to be honest, it is moments like this that have led me to adopt Las Vegas as *mi varrio*. I mean, here was an *American*, in 1994, who was thankful for something and looking forward to something else. So now I affectionately exchange stories of Vegas' little quirks with my fellow homies. (I chuckle over the legendary teddy bear in the gift shop at Caesars Palace that was reputedly sold

500 times. Every night, it seems, some john would buy it for a hooker. Every morning, a hooker would bring it back for cash. That night another john would buy it for another hooker – and thus the cycle continued until Herr Teddy, that fuzzy emblem of middle-aged desire, became irretrievably shop-worn.) I also defend my adopted hometown against its detractors – a great many of whom are disconsolate colleagues of mine down at the University – lost souls whom I must count among those who are *not* looking forward to moving up from 'food' to 'cocktail', who do not arise from their slumber thanking their lucky stars to have escaped Mom and Dad and fucking Ithaca.

These exiles, it seems, find Las Vegas lacking in culture. (Define culture!) They think it is all about money, which, I always agree, is by far the worst way of discriminating among individuals, except for all the others. They also deplore the fact that Las Vegas exploits people's weaknesses – although, in my view, Vegas rather theatrically *fails* to exploit that most plangent American weakness, for being parented into senility. Which is probably why so many regard Vegas as an unfit atmosphere in which to raise children – although judging by my students, the town turns out an amazingly resilient and insouciant brand of American adolescent, one whose penchant for body decoration seems to me a healthier way of theatricalising one's lack of prospects than the narcotics that performed this function for my generation.

Most of all, however, I suspect that my unhappy colleagues are appalled by the fact that Vegas presents them with a flat-line social hierarchy – that, having ascended from 'food' to 'cocktail' in Las Vegas, there is hardly anywhere else to go (except, perhaps, up to 'magician'), and being a professor in this environment does not feel nearly as special as it might in Cambridge or Bloomington – simply because money, in Las Vegas, is *just* money. You can make it here, but there are no socially sanctioned forms of status to ennoble one's *having* made it – nor any predetermined socio-cultural agendas that one might pursue as a privilege of having been so ennobled.

Thus, in the absence of vertical options, one is pretty much thrown back onto one's own cultural resources, and, for me, this has not been the worst place to be thrown. At least I have begun to wonder if the privilege of living in a community with a culture does not outweigh the absence of a 'cultural community' and, to a certain extent, explain its absence. (Actually, it's not so bad. My *TLS* comes in the mail every week, regular as clockwork, and the other day I took down my grandfather's

Cicero and read for nearly an hour without anyone breaking down my door and forcing me to listen to Wayne Newton.)

This deficiency of *haute bourgeois* perks, I should note, also confuses visiting Easterners whom I have docented down the Strip. So attentive are they to signifiers of status and exclusivity that they become restless and frustrated. The long, lateral blend of Vegas iconography unrolls before them, and they are looking for the unmarked door through which the cognoscenti pass. They want the 'secret Vegas'. They can't believe that there are no private gaming rooms where Bruce Willis and Marky Mark may risk their ill-gotten gains. Not that these sophisticates *believe* in celebrity, of course. But still, the idea that people with Names must gamble in public, with the rest of us, somehow offends their sense of order – and mitigates their aspirations as well. I suspect.

In any case, when visiting culturati actually start shivering in the horizontal flux, I take them to one of the two restaurants in town where tank-tops are (sort of) discouraged. This is the best I can do to restore their sense of propriety, because the 'secret of Vegas' is that there are *no* secrets. And there are only two rules: (1) post the odds, and (2) treat everybody the same. Just as one might in a democracy (what a concept!), and this deficiency of secrets and economy of rules drives writers crazy! They come here to write about Vegas. They are trained in depth-analysis. They have ripped the lid off seamy scandals by getting behind the scenes, and, thus, Las Vegas is invisible to them. They see the lights, of course, but they end up writing stories about white people who are so unused to regulating their own behaviour that they gamble away the farm, get drunk, throw up on their loafers and wind up in custody within six hours of their arrival. Or they write profiles of the colourful Runyonesque characters they meet in casinos, oblivious to the fact that such characters populate half the bar rooms in America – that, in truth, they need only have driven a few blocks for their 'colorful characters', had they been inclined to transgress the rigid stratifications that (in *their* hometowns) stack the classes like liqueurs in a dessert drink.

America, in other words, is a very poor lens through which to view Las Vegas, while Las Vegas is a wonderful lens through which to view America. What is hidden elsewhere exists here in quotidian visibility. So when you fly out of Las Vegas to, say, Milwaukee, the absences imposed by repression are like holes in your vision. They become breathtakingly perceptible, and as a consequence, there is no better place than Las Vegas for a traveller to feel at home. The town has a quick, feral glamour that is hard to localise – and it arises, I think, out of the suppression of social differences rather than their exacerbation. Thus the whole city floats on a sleek *frisson* of anxiety and promise that those of us addicted to such distraction must otherwise induce by motion or medication.

Moreover, since I must regularly venture out of Vegas onto the bleak savannahs of high culture, and there, like an ageing gigolo, generate bodily responses to increasingly abject objects of desire, there is nothing as bracing as the prospect of flying home, of swooping down into that ardent explosion of lights in the heart of the pitch-black desert – of coming home to the only indigenous visual culture on the North American continent, a town bereft of white walls, grey wool carpets, and Barcelona chairs – where there is everything to see and not a single pretentious object demanding to be scrutinised.

I remember one particular evening in the spring. I was flying back from Washington, DC after serving on an NEA panel. For four solid days, I had been seated on a wooden chair in a dark room looking at racks of slides, five at a time. Blam, blam, blam, blam, blam, *ad infinitum.* All hope departed somewhere near the end of the second day, and I started counting popular iconography (skulls, little houses, little boats, altars, etc). By the end of the third day, despair had become a very real option, but, finally, we selected the correct number of winners – and a number of these actually won. The rest won the privilege of having their awards overturned by a higher court on the grounds of propriety.

Anyway, the moment I stepped off the plane, I sat down in the terminal to play video poker. Basically, I was doing the same thing I had been doing in Washington: looking at banks of five images, one after another, interpreting finite permutations of a limited iconography, looking for a winner. However, sitting there at the slot machine, I was comfortable in the knowledge that Vegas cheats you fair – that, unlike the rest of America (and Washington in particular), the odds are posted and easily calculable. I *knew* how much of a chance I had to win. It was slim, of course, but it was a real chance nevertheless, not some vague promise of parental benevolence contingent on my behaviour.

And in the reality of that chance, Vegas lives – in those fluttery moments of faint but rising hope, in the possibility of wonder, in the swell of desire while the dice are still bouncing, just before the card flips face-up. And win or lose, you always have that instant of genuine, *justifiable* hope. It is always there. Even though we know the rules governing random events are always overtaken by the law of large numbers, there is always that window of opportunity, that statistical crazy zone, before this happens, when *anything* can happen. And, what's more, if you win, you win! You can take it home. You cannot be deemed unworthy after the fact – as we all were in Washington, where we played our hearts out and never had a fucking chance. So right there in the airport, I could make a little wager, and there was a real chance that luck and foolish courage might, just for the moment, just for a couple of bucks, override the quagmire of status and virtue in which we daily languish. And if I got *really* lucky, I might move up from food to cocktail. Hey, don't laugh. It could happen.

RUBÉN ORTIZ-TORRES

Rubén Ortiz-Torres, Santo Niño/Holy Kid, *Guanajuato, Mexico, 1991, 7.9x9.4cm*

LUIS ALFARO

The Three Mexican Musketeers

The Three Mexican Musketeers. That's what we were. Small-time change in a big slot machine of a city. I worshipped my brother, Jaime, like little kids worshipped Cassius Clay or Lew Alcindor. Loved him because he always opened the back door of the bus so that I could sneak on. The Third Musketeer was our neighbour, Gabriel, whose dad was gone by the time we longed to go to ball games with absent guys they called *father*.

We befriended Gabriel after his dog Brandy died; we felt sorry and helped dig out a grave in his backyard on Valencia Street. Stole plywood from the Pico-Union projects construction site and made a big cross like we had seen in a stations-of-the-cross Tijuana trip. My brother gave him our favourite 45-rpm single to play on the portable bought at Zody's. He hugged Gabriel like a father when he started crying in the backyard as we put up that big old cross over his buried dog, while the portable wailed, 'Ooh Brandy, you're a fine girl. What a good wife you would be'.

After that, Gabriel was our friend, even though he ate non-Mexican food like waffles. But we had things in common. He was fatherless to a long-ago divorce and we were fatherless to a lost-cause dad who spent his days at the Club Jalisco on Union Street. We were a gang of misfits. Different from the 18th Street boys, 'cause we were nice and we didn't sniff no glue. We played out our adventures on the streets of downtown Los Angeles before the greysuits took over Broadway.

Downtown was our backyard. *El centro* was the place to run through education electives that weren't offered at Tenth Street Elementary. Stuff like Heavy Petting 101 or Advanced Shoplifting on Olvera Street. That summer we almost lost my brother to a girl who lived in the Maravilla projects, who Gabriel and I thought was, like, just *all right*. Her name was Lorraine and the only thing cool about her was her *chola* eyebrows, which were shaped like Elizabeth Taylor's in *Cleopatra*. Luckily, my brother got bored with the bus trips through East LA and returned to our Musketeer downtown adventures.

One Saturday, we scoured the neighbourhood for soda bottles. Turned them in for the five-cent deposit so we could pay for the bus fare and a kid's admission to the movies. We stood in front of the Tower Theater at Seventh and Broadway looking for somebody who would pretend to be our parent and buy us tickets for an R-rated kung fu movie.

All of a sudden, Gabriel started to cry. Not just cry but sob, like he saw a devil. We walked around the corner, down near the racing-form stand. My brother, our caretaker, pulled up his T-shirt to wipe Gabriel's face and held his hand like in those pictures of little Madeleine and her friends in Paris.

'I saw my dad.'

That's what he said, just like that. Saw his dad drive by in front of the Tower Theater and wave at him. And I just didn't get it. I told him that if I had seen my dad driving by, I would've run up and gotten in that car and made him buy me dinner at The Pantry and drive me home, instead of having to get on that rowdy No 26 bus where somebody always plays their Marvin Gaye way too loud.

We stood in front of the Tower Theater and waited for Gabriel's dad for about an hour. Missed the first showing of *The Chinese Connection*. I prayed we wouldn't be late for *Enter the Dragon*. The thing about Chinese kung fu movies is that if you miss the first five minutes, you miss the whole reason why they spend the rest of the movie fighting; besides, I couldn't rush Gabriel, who was waiting for another chance to see his long-lost father.

Right when it seemed we were going to die because the previews were already on, that old green station wagon pulled up in front of the theatre. Gabriel's dad smiled all nice like he'd been gone only a few minutes, like he just went out to buy milk or something.

Gabriel didn't even say good-bye. Didn't even give us his movie entrance money or nothing. Just hopped in the car and drove off like he'd waited all his life in front of the Tower Theater for his dad to just drive by and pick him up.

And that was the last we saw of Gabriel. We went in and watched all of *Enter the Dragon* and did not have a clue as to why Bruce Lee was angry and who we were supposed to be cheering for.

Later that night, Gabriel's mom came over and started asking where Gabriel was. My mom brought her into our room and she looked terrified, wearing that *tamale* apron and her hair up in curlers. When my brother told her that he went with his dad, she fell down fainting, crying, sobbing, screaming. Went crazy right in front of us. My mother and father tried to pick her up off the floor as she screamed that *he'd stolen her son*. I told my mom to call the police, but no one did. In our neighbourhood, no one ever called the police. Sometimes you'd call the ambulance or the morgue. But there were too many *illegales* in our neighbourhood, my dad included, to have the police snooping around our block looking for wetbacks. Besides, by the time she came over that night, Gabriel and his dad were way past the border and deep into the night on a Mexican highway. And that was the night that the voice went out of Gabriel's mom. She never spoke again. At least not in public.

Gabriel returned home the year we started eighth grade, but there was no more room for the Third Musketeer. We were eating up the American Apple Pie like there was no tomorrow. He was *Mr TJ*, *Mr Taco* to us. Came back speaking Spanish and wearing *huaraches*. We walked through junior high in our 70s platforms, talking *Soul Train* dialects. I didn't have time for no Third Musketeer. Once, I saw Gabriel at a bus stop on the way to school. In true junior-high fashion, I pretended not to see him. I was into noon dances and Minnie Riperton and he was hanging out with Jose Chavez and the soccer club.

But I'll tell you one thing. Even though we'd never admit it, we Two Musketeers spent about six months after that incident hanging out in front of the Tower Theater, wondering, and maybe hoping that a green station wagon was cruising down Broadway looking for us. Spent more Saturday afternoons standing on Seventh Street with stolen cigarettes dangling from our mouths, wondering about the *ranchos* in Mexico. Praying that there was an absent father looking for a couple of Musketeers on a street corner.

I would have missed the previews for that one.

The Shrine Auditorium

In the fifth grade, my brother and I were sent on a yellow school bus to see a performance of the ever-popular *Barber of Seville*. Before I go on, let me just say that I do not believe that there's anything wrong with the *Barber of Seville*, or with opera in general. But in the fifth grade, the obsessions of our youth were the voices of the Jackson Five. *Nobody ever asked us where we wanted to go on our field trips.*

My brother echoed my sentiment that day we took home the trip slip to be signed by our parents: 'Fuck Figaro, man'. Even now, I think of that phrase every time I see Placido collect his classical Grammy. Nevertheless, the night before our big field trip, we spent it singing but one word: Figaro. At the dinner table with mashed potatoes in our mouths we sang; Figaro, Figaro, Figaro. Right up until our mother shouted, '*Ya callense con esa cancion!*' Maybe other kids would have enjoyed such a visit to this grand concert hall. But every Saturday morning my brother and I would walk to the USC mall directly across the street from the Shrine Auditorium. We were definitely feeling gypped if this was going to be the only field trip of the year.

'Why can't we go far?' my brother would say.

'What's far?' I would ask.

'I don't know, far. That's not far.'

Years later, this dialogue served as the cue for my running away from home. (Unfortunately, I ran away to Echo Park, about five minutes from downtown. Let's just say that my hori-

zons have expanded since then.)

I was the shy, quiet Alfaro. My brother was the best pal and buddy to all. A combination sports jock, boy-most-likely-to, dare-taker, girl-kisser, all-around practical joker. I studied and concentrated on winning free *Highlander* workbooks with my conformity while my brother perfected the art of heavy petting.

The day of the field trip, little Jose Gonzales, who lived down the street, started in on us for bringing burritos. He laughed and screamed, 'Where'd you get your lunches, Tijuana?'

I held my brother back and begged him not to speak the unspeakable. You see, Mrs Gonzales, little Jose's mother, got taken away on a Saturday morning long ago. When in a crazed rage she ran down the street, naked and crying, and asking to speak to the president of the United States. After that, nobody mentioned Mrs Gonzales again. As if she had never existed. As if she never baked Explorer Scout cupcakes, or went to PTA meetings, or read at Sunday mass or helped with the Stations of the Cross. Never again did we hear about Mrs Gonzales. Like broken fingers and stillborn babies, you kind of just forgot about her. Except my brother, of course. It seems that he was almost always going to mention Mrs Gonzales to little Jose, but we didn't altar boy the 6.00am mass all summer at our parish, Immaculate Conception, to blow our chance at heaven on one stupid little remark.

Our teacher, Mrs Polka, notices our fifth-grade conflict. In her black mini-skirt and white knee-high boots, she checks her lipstick in a very sexy, non-threatening Angie Dickinson sort of way and coos, 'Jose Gonzales, quiet please'.

Inside the Shrine Auditorium, what seem to be thousands of children from Unified School Districts throughout the universe shriek and scream as they test the building's echo system. I imagine uptight little opera singers with big voices, muttering in the wings, 'Oh shit'.

As we file into our row, my brother and I lead the class to our seats, which is, I guess, one of the pleasures of being an A for Alfaro. But a nervous twinge sweeps over me when I notice that row two is being led by little Jose, a G for Gonzales. He sits directly behind us with a wicked smile on his face.

The lights in the auditorium begin to fade. A fifth-grade hush, with a few boos and scattered giggles, and the lights on the stage brighten and the opera begins. We are not even five minutes into it when little Jose Gonzales whispers, 'It smells like burritos in here', and then that all-time stupid nervous giggle – half nostril, half contracted throat. *I hate asthma kids*.

My brother starts to tense up and I start to get nervous. His nostrils flare and he begins to brush back his hair like he always does when he gets angry. It is at these times in my youth that I sought the solace of a higher source. I try to pray a novena without the beads and hope that God will forgive me and intercede. But then it happens. I should have known that eventually it would.

In the cavernous darkness of the Shrine Auditorium, my

brother and I hear, 'How does your fat mom squeeze into the kitchen to make burritos anyway?'

It is followed by an even more strained asthma giggle. It is asked with such cruelty that I feel it pierce my heart. A getting-caught-shoplifting kind of feeling. At that moment I learn many things: What do I know? What do I know? I know that there is no heaven. I know that my brother tries and that his good nature fails him. I know that bad people, early on, win more than they lose. I know that our lives will never be the same. I know that I altar-boyed for nothing. I know that God doesn't hear very well. I know that things hurt because they are true. And all of this I knew because we did have a fat mom. A big-thighed mother who waddled around the house and smothered us with so much affection that we loved her exactly the way she was. A mom who tried all the diets and laughed them off as we sat in the car at Foster Freeze on Huntington Drive eating chocolate sundaes. A mom whom I always felt I could sink into.

The beginning of the end is near. I can tell by the fidgety hand as it makes its way to the hairline. Then I hear my brother's voice as clear as if I had heard God's voice in the heavens, 'I'd rather have a fat mom than a crazy naked mom anyday'.

My heart does a very fast *cucaracha* dance. I look behind me and I see it register on the face of little Jose Gonzales. A look that should be added to the *Seven Faces of Death* video. Tears roll down his cheeks and the sadness of a million summers ending rolls over me. I remember an article in one of my many *Highlander* workbooks. *Why is there meanness?* I swear to myself that I will never pray again.

A squashed, breathless scream escapes from little Jose's mouth and he jumps on my brother's back. A few children shout in high-pitched voices. My brother rises from his seat and begins to beat the holy crap out of little Jose Gonzales. The orchestra rises to a crescendo. Children start to run for the aisles. A collective chorus of cheers and whistles echo off the walls. A chaos breaks out in row five. Our row. Some boys join in. Some allied with the Alfaro camp, some with the Gonzales. Little girls cry and run down the aisles. I look towards the stage and even the opera people are staring at us. The Barber of Seville himself has walked towards the lip of the stage to see what is going on.

I look to my left and see the dreaded black mini-skirt and the white knee-high boots racing toward us. I lean into my brother and beg him to stop and I look into his face and see that he is smiling. He's smiling. How can he be smiling? I think my brother likes this. In fact, I can see that he's enjoying himself very much. This is the one event my brother has been waiting for all of his eleven years. He's obviously peaking early. My brother is having a *moment*.

Mrs Polka reaches over me and I see her bright red painted nails dig into my brother's arm. He screams but continues to punch the Gonzales camp. Then I see the scratch on my brother's arm from that fifth-grade teacher's nails and I scream. She digs in again and this time strikes gold when the blood drips down from my brother's skin. And then the world of my brother, Jaime Alfaro Junior, ended as quickly as it had begun. My brother's arm comes up off of little Jose Gonzales, stretches to an open palm and lands almost perfectly on Mrs Polka's face.

There is an audible gasp. For a moment it seems that the world has stopped. One big 'oh-oh' echoes through the cavernous auditorium. Mrs Polka is stunned. Paralysed. The blood rushes to her face and it contorts into that of a Disney villainess. I face my brother just in time to watch him end his aria with a finale so inspired that I shiver. He arches up his eleven-year-old body as far as it will go, purses his cheeks and dead aims a wad of spit that hits a bullseye on Mrs Polka's cheek.

A thousand school children cheer and scream and I stagger towards a seat dazed and embarrassed at the spectacle that I have just witnessed. It is opera at its finest, no doubt. And I am moved to do what any opera lover would do; I break into tears. There is nothing else I can think of to do to acknowledge the performance. I mean, applause would seem cheap.

I sit in row five and just start to bawl. I bawl for the lack of a heaven. I bawl for the feeling that I'll never be a boy again. I even bawl that Santa doesn't exist anymore, even though I've known that for years. I watch my brother being dragged down the long Shrine Auditorium aisle and I think, *how sad*. How sad that he gave such a great performance and to what? The peons of the Los Angeles Unified School District.

As he is being led away by a couple of principals and a mini-skirted fifth-grade teacher with spit on her face, he is bleeding from the arm, kicking and screaming, and *llorando* and laughing like I had never seen him laugh and cry before. And I know I have seen the performance of a lifetime.

The Doll

We used to have this *Virgen de Guadalupe* doll. Every time you connected her to an outlet, she would turn and bless all sides of the room.

We bought her on one of my dad's surprise drunken trips to Tijuana. He would come home from the race track at about midnight, wake us up, get us dressed and we would all hop into the station wagon. My mom drove and my dad lowered the seat in the back and he slept with us. My grandmother, *La Abuela*, lived in one of the *colonias*. She hated our 3.00am visits. But you see, *blood is thicker than water, family is greater than friends, and Our Lady watches over all of us.*

When I was ten, I gave the *Virgen* doll to my *Tia Ofelia*. My *Tia Ofelia* lived across the street with my *Tia Tita*, who lived with my *Tio Tony*, who lived next door to my *Tia Romie*. Back in those days, everybody was either a *tia* or a *tio*. They lived in a big, beautiful two-storey house with a balcony overlooking the street below. We were crowded in by downtown skyscrapers, packs of roving *cholos*, the newly built Convention Center on Pico, and portable *tamale* stands. But our families always managed to live together, because we all knew: *blood is thicker than water, family is greater than friends, and Our Lady watches over all of us*.

My *tia* lived on the second floor, and on the first lived the 18th Street Gang. There was *Smiley, Sleepy, La Sadgirl* and a bunch of other homeboys who hung out in the front yard playing Bloodstones' *Natural High*. They split, like *cucarachas* exposed to light, at the sight of a cop car slowly cruising through our Pico-Union neighbourhood, like tourists on Hollywood Boulevard.

My *tia*, she hated *cholos* and she would spit out, from the window, the seeds of grapes she ate, just to annoy them. She was like all of my relatives back then. A grape picker from Delano, California. She claimed to have dated Cesar Chavez, and to know everyone in McFarland, Tulare and Visalia Counties – the farm worker capitals of *el mundo*.

I couldn't call her a liar, because she had *breast cancer*. My mom told us this in a voice reserved for nights when we didn't want to wake up my dad after one of his drunken soccer celebrations. Doctors at County General took away her tits in hopes of driving away *La Bruja Maldita*, who was slowly eating at her insides. When she was feeling okay, my *tia* would tell me stories about the farm worker movement and picking cherries one summer.

The day I brought her the rotating Our Lady doll, I knew she was in pain. I knew I probably should have waited, but I asked her quite innocently if I could see her chest. She slapped me hard on the face, calling me a *malcriado*. While she sobbed, her hand searched for medication. I felt so bad that day. Even I could feel *La Bruja Maldita* eating at my heart. I never got the nerve to go back up there again.

Weeks went by and my *tia* continued to rock in her chair. When the weeks turned to months, she slowly started to forget us. People would walk by and offer up a *buenas tardes Señora*, but you could tell she was having trouble remembering faces. My grandmother sent a crate of grapes to help her remember but nothing worked. My mom and my *Tia Romie* said that my *Tia Ofelia* was becoming a baby, *otra vez*. The *Bruja Maldita* ate at her bones and slowly she started to melt like the GI Joes that my brother and I set fire to with burning *tamale* leaves. Her cheeks caved in like the plaster *calaveras* that you could buy at the border on *el dia de los muertos*. And one day, on my way home from school, I looked up, and she was gone.

Phones rang, food poured in, little envelopes with $20 bills. Hysterical screams from aunts on a Mexico-to-LA party line. Dramatic uncles wept openly and the tears of my relatives were covered with huge veils that they wore to church. My grandmother, *La Abuela*, got into the drama when, at the burial, she jumped onto the coffin, screaming.

A few weeks later, the Crips drove by and shouted, 'Chump Mother Fuckers. Greasy Assed Messicans. Go back to Teehuana'. And they firebombed the 18th Street Gang on the bottom floor. A great ball of fire and light filled the downtown sky, and for just a moment there, it was better than fireworks at Dodger Stadium. But it lasted for just a moment. Then seriousness took over. Followed by weeks of tears and sorrows and that same story about my *tia*'s escape from the second storey. Crazy relatives would start crying every time you turned on the burner on the stove.

Smiley, Sleepy, y La Sadgirl died, but we couldn't go to the funeral because my dad said they were *perros desgraciados*. Instead, we rummaged through charred remains looking for usable clothes and my *tia*'s collection of Vicki Carr records.

My brother found what was left of the Our Lady doll and he used her head for BB-gun practice. My mom cried because the memory of my *Tia Ofelia* would now be an empty lot where bums would piss and tires would grow. Every day she watered a little flower she had planted in the memory of my *Tia Ofelia*, until the Community Redevelopment Agency built the Pico-Union Projects over her memory.

When I was 18, I met this guy with a rotating Our Lady doll. He bought it in Mexico; so, of course, I fell in love.

His skin was white, he ate broccoli and he spoke like the actors in a TV series. He was every *Partridge Family/Brady Bunch* episode rolled into one. He taught me many things: how to kiss like the French, lick an earlobe, dance in the dark. Once, my grandmother, *La Abuela*, sent us lovers a crate of grapes. We took off our clothes, smashed the grapes all over our bodies and licked them off each other.

When he left, the *Bruja Maldita*'s hand replaced his in my heart. And she pounded on it. She laughed like Mexican mothers laugh while hanging *la ropa* on a clothes line. My sorrow was so strong but I kept it hidden with smiles that were like the veils my aunts wore at Immaculate Conception church. But my sorrow bled through, like stigmata, like rushing waters, and my relatives would say, '*Ay mijo*, don't you understand? *Blood is thicker than water, family is greater than friends, and that old Virgen, Our Lady, she just watches over all of us . . .*'

Scrap Recycling Project with American Ingenuity (Group B), *1995, wood, high-pressure laminate, approx 406.4x182.3cm;*
OVERLEAF: Abandoned House #2, *1995, mixed media, 83.8x108x121cm*

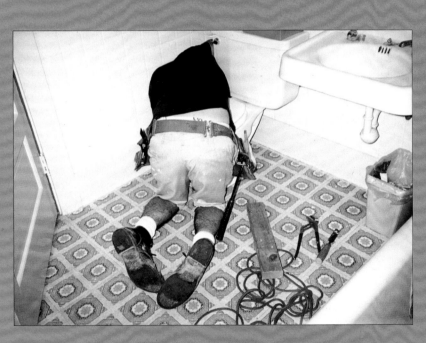

Philosophy of Work, *1992, four c-prints, plastic frames,*
8.9x12.7cm each

FROM ABOVE, L to R: Empty #24, 1992, Empty #3, 1992, Empty
#21, 1992, Empty #8, 1992, c-prints, 76.2x50.8cm each

SAFE AS HOUSES
Karen Klabin

If you've seen Sam Durant's art, you know it has something to do with building, with tinkering, with making physical changes to bring about emotional changes. You see a culture constantly in the process of adding rooms, fixing toilets, building bookcases, designing houses – looking outwards to solve an inner crisis. You see people's desperate attempts to stave off chaos. It might be noble were it not pathetic, which is what makes Durant's work so funny, and so sad.

I happened to be in the midst of reading a biography of the architect/curator Philip Johnson (the great promoter of Modern architecture in the US) when I first saw Durant's work. At the centre of his exhibition were five battered, crappy models of Los Angeles's Case Study Program houses (most built during the 1950s), which were grounded in the Modernist doctrine of affordability through simplicity in design. Durant's 'Abandoned Houses', made from cheap cardboard and foamcore, were riddled with holes and graffiti, and mostly barren, save for an overturned miniature chair. At the time, because I was immersed in Johnson's life and thinking what a distasteful elitist prig he is (colouring my opinion of Modernist architecture in general), my heart swelled at the idea that Durant was making an ironic jab at the coldness of Modern design. However, as I later learned, there was more at work than mere irony.

'With [the Case Study Houses], it was how utopian ideas in Modern design mutated into the culture, into corporate identity,' explains Durant, whose ideas were also shaped by Austrian architect Adolf Loos's 1908 essay 'Ornament and Crime', which he read as a student. Loos's thesis, a significant influence on Modern theory, was that ornamentation was used in design – for architecture, clothing, furniture – as a means of masking the mediocrity of culture and social conditions. His outlook, however, was utopian; the removal of ornamentation was supposed to eventually result in sounder structures, both in the literal, physical sense and in the figurative (a cultural and socio-economic context). Were it only that simple.

To Durant, the 'abandonment' of those model houses symbolises not merely the abandonment of Modernism's style, but, more importantly, its highly Socialistic founding tenets. The irony is that this architecture of asceticism quickly became a fashion statement for rich folks with an eye for towering modesty. (Puritanism in architecture would seem a natural extension of American aesthetics. Has there ever been another nation that so fiercely champions the excesses of wealth and then turns on its heel to self-flagellate?)

In his art, Durant's beliefs about the socio-economic underpinnings of design theory appear to collide – some of them seemingly born of hope and empathy, others of crusty cynicism. Having worked in construction and as a carpenter, Durant says he is sincere in his understanding of, and interest in, the motivation to build. When asked about the Case Study houses, he talks in Marxist lingo about the consequences of mass production: 'As a worker, the further away you get from the totality of your product, the more alienated you become.' You are also usually no closer to obtaining that product for yourself. The Program was supposedly taking the lead in the demand for affordable housing for the growing postwar American middle class. Yet the faces looking out of those steel-and-glass aeries were not ones that would ever be wrinkled by the trifling matters of everyday life, such as making ends meet.

The logical conclusion to Durant's premise is that if you feel alienated from the totality of your work, it is reasonable on a psychological level to tinker with little projects in order to preserve some sense of achievement in your life. The modern world was supposed to bring people closer to material gain, but what was it doing for psychic stability? 'There's a peculiar American tendency towards self-reliance,' Durant observes. 'Our Zeitgeist or ethos is that we're a country of individuals. There isn't a big social net here, and the way that translates is that you're supposed to fix your own emotional life. For a lot of people, their identity is tied into what they do. Working is the way they maintain their emotional life. And self-esteem and self-confidence tend to get caught up in how productive they [perceive themselves to be].'

So with all his sympathy for alienated workers, for desperate tinkerers, for people who have ceased to make their economic or cultural contribution, why is it that in his installations they are represented as pathetic schlubs? Durant's reply is that while he is sincere in his understanding of the psychological context, he is also aware of the irony in a cultural context. 'My relationship to this stuff is very ambivalent', he admits. 'I have very complex feelings about it. I am not going to make a moral judgment. If you make a political statement, it shuts down the work. It becomes a lesson. I'd rather present conflicting information'.

OPPOSITE, FROM ABOVE: We're Remodeling, *1992, installation at Bliss, Pasadena, CA;* 1000 Coffees, *1992, Styrofoam and paper cups, dimensions variable*

ABOVE: Scrap Recycling Project with American Ingenuity (Group C), *1995, wood, high-pressure laminate, approx 304.8x203.2cm; PAGE 30:* Sitting, Problem Solving, Identity, etc, *1995, four drawings, pencil on paper, 72.4x57.2cm each; PAGE 31, FROM ABOVE:* Entertainment Center (Subject: Psychological, Self-Help, Love, Relationships, Do-It-Yourself), *1994, plywood, books, 169.5x179.7x45.8cm;* Coffee Table (Games People Play, I'm OK You're OK), *1994, books, glass, particle board, 36.1x101.6x71.1cm*

MARK BENNETT

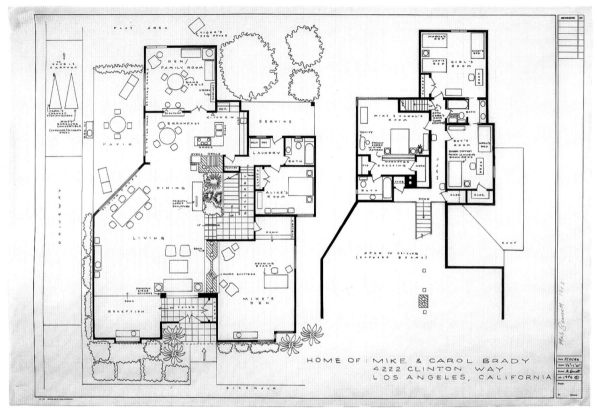

Home of Mike and Carol Brady, 1986-95, ink and pencil on graph vellum, 70x91.4cm

The Brady Bunch House *This split-level contemporary house, located at 4222 Clinton Way, Los Angeles, features three bedrooms, three bathrooms, and a maid's room for Alice. A double-door entry leads to a dramatic cathedral-ceilinged living/dining room, where Mike and Carol entertain guests and occasionally have parent/child pow-wows. Mike's den is separated from the living room by a brick fireplace and adjustable louver shutters – permanently closed when Greg temporarily made it his 'crash pad'. The kitchen is an ideal workplace for the two cooks, Carol and Alice, who often work together to prepare the meals. Done in birch cabinetry and orange Formica countertops, the kitchen features a dishwasher, refrigerator/freezer, double ovens and an indoor barbecue grill. A cosy den, behind the serving counter, houses the family's entertainment centre: hi-fi, colour television, game table. Alice's room, near the laundry room/service porch, contains louver-door closets and an adjoining bath. A slate patio runs the width of the house and is accessible through sliding doors. A detached, double carport, which stores the Bradys' Plymouth autos (Mike's sporty convertible and Carol's sensible station wagon) sits at the back of the property, along with a children's play area and Tiger's dog house. The second floor, reached by the distinctive cantilevered staircase, boasts two children's rooms with a shared bath, and a master suite with dressing area and bath. There is a stairway up to a roomy attic, which later became a bedroom as first Greg, and then Marcia grew into their teens.*

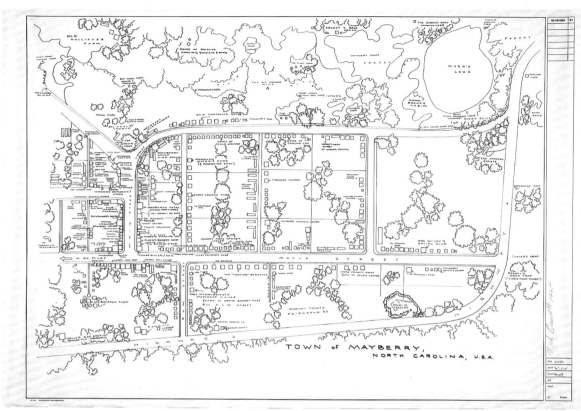

Town of Mayberry, 1989-95, ink and pencil on graph vellum, 61x91.4cm

Town of Mayberry *Entering the peaceful town of Mayberry, probably via Highway Six, past the sign that says 'Welcome to Mayberry, the Friendly Town', the motorist might first stop at Wally's Gas Station for a fill-up and soda pop. Lush trees, clean air, Emma Brand's homey cabin overlooking Myer's Lake – you would think you had driven into an environment of endless summer days and southern charm. It's true. Drive past the County Fairgrounds and the old Palmerton Drive-In Theater, take a right on Elm Street and you are heading towards town. At 411 Elm, you can wave at Barney's bachelor digs: Mrs Mendelbright's Rooming House. A right on Maple will take you past Sheriff Andy Taylor's modest home and the sweet smells of Aunt Bee's culinary delights. Clara Edwards lives next door, Nurse Peggy (her house was later sold to Helen Crump) lives down the street, and two blocks further is Mayberry Water & Power. Heading south on Maple and hanging a quick right on Main Street will take the casual tourist into the hub of Mayberry activity: Foley's Market, Floyd's Barber Shop, the courthouse, the Bluebird Diner. It is very quaint here – brick buildings with flower boxes and street benches and citizens playing chequers in front of the Mayberry Hotel. Weaver's Department Store offers the shopper the ultimate in dry goods, and the Snappy Lunch has daily specials such as lemon phosphates. You could live here. Everyone offers a friendly hello, a warm smile, a covered dish to welcome you to the community. A Greyhound bus stops every day on Main Street and traffic is almost non-existent. You will see all the locals on Sunday at the All Soul's Church; Rafe Hollister will sing a hymn and the Morrison sisters might invite you home for Sunday dinner and a fresh batch of their home-brew. There are favourite fishing holes, the old Johnson Mine and the spooky Rimshaw House to explore. If you get bored, you can talk to Sarah, the phone operator. And if it gets really stale, there's always Mr Pilot.*

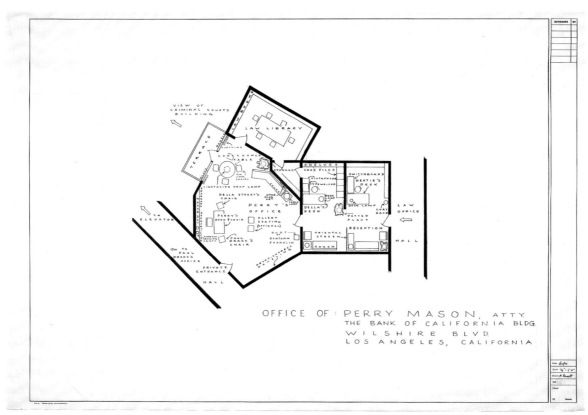

Office of Perry Mason, 1995, ink and pencil on graph vellum, 61x91.4cm

Office of Perry Mason *When a man is the most celebrated attorney in Los Angeles, he can afford a posh law office on Wilshire Boulevard in the Bank of California building. Picture yourself being accused of murder and strolling into the reception area of Perry Mason, Attorney at Law. To the left, modern, functional upholstered couches; to the right, Gertie, the street-wise blonde at the switchboard. Beyond a black-lacquered Japanese screen and potted philodendron is the desk of Perry's right hand and legal secretary, Miss Della Street. Separating the switchboard and Della's work station is a row of black filing cabinets, filled with some of the most celebrated case files in the annals of the Los Angeles justice system. On the tasteful couch with matching chair and end table, Miss Street will dry your tears, fix you a perfect cup of coffee, and reassure you. At the designated appointment time, you are lead through a single four-foot mahogany door into the Berber-carpeted sanctum: pecky-cypress panelling; an angular, low-slung white couch; Finn Juhl conference table and chairs; floor-to-ceiling glass panels with a terraced view. You realise that not only has Mr Mason hired a decorator, but he has also raided the high-end Baker, Knapp & Tubbs showroom. A snooty piece of art (relief-carved stone) hangs behind the couch and a bronze sculpture rests on a pedestal by the door. A Lightolier chandelier holds court above the conference table, just before the entrance to Perry's fully stocked law library. The desk is a sleek, modern peg-boarded affair, a floating veneered top holding a simple leather fountain-pen set. Behind this, a credenza stands against the wall, holding books encased between two globe-shaped bookends. To the left is a secret entrance/exit door, often used by private investigator Paul Drake, who has an office down the hall. From these surroundings you realise that the cup of coffee Della has handed you might cost more than you can afford.*

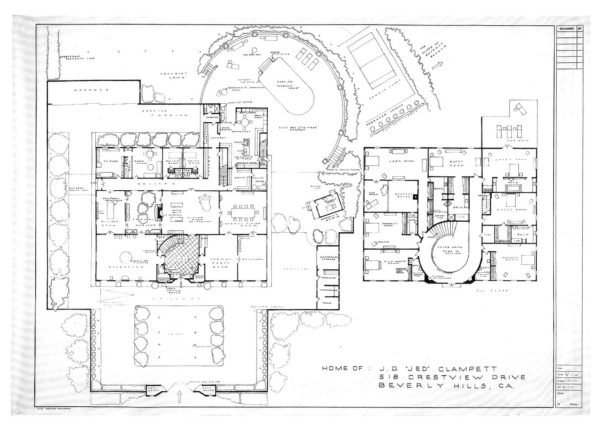

Home of JD 'Jed' Clampett, 1987-95, ink and pencil on graph vellum, 61x91.4cm

The Clampett Mansion *The Clampett's home, at 518 Crestview Drive in Beverly Hills, is regal French Regency with impressive gates and dual guard houses at the entrance. With manicured lawns and topiary box-hedges, this 27-room spread also has a much-used motor court, a swimming pool, tennis courts, a billiard room and enough bedrooms for all of Ellie Mae's 'critters'. Drive up to the front door, step out of Miss Jane Hathaway's red Dodge Coronet convertible (she trades it in for a new one every year, it seems) and ring the door chimes that Granny and Jethro thought were ghosts. Once inside, you step down into an oval foyer, complete with built-in pedestal urns, a fleur-de-lys tiled, diamond-patterned floor (perfect for hoe-downs or ballroom dancing) and a sweeping, curved staircase that makes even Jed's simple duds look runway-perfect. Straight ahead is the 'parlor' or living room, with courtin' couches, a fireplace separating two sets of French doors, and a baby grand piano for visiting cousin Jethrene to play. The kitchen is a chef's paradise: double ovens, dual range tops, Sub Zero refrigerator-freezer, a laundry room, and a breakfast nook with seating for four. Step outside to a glamorous pavilion high above Beverly Hills and check out the swimming pool, with Grecian-goddess figurine fountains, an elaborate set of upholstered patio furniture, and Granny's lye-soap kettle, simmering on low flame. Enjoy the solitude of this aquatic setting before Jethro turns it into a three-minute car wash. Upstairs, there are countless bedroom suites, all with distinctive starburst-patterned closet doors and elaborate bathrooms (surely with sunken tubs), all off a circular balcony that sweeps around the foyer. The Clampetts did not settle well into their house at first. They ruined the front-lawn sprinkler system trying to raise crops. And the sight of Jed whittling near the front door caused the neighbours to think the hired help had run amok. No wonder Mrs Drysdale wanted to move.*

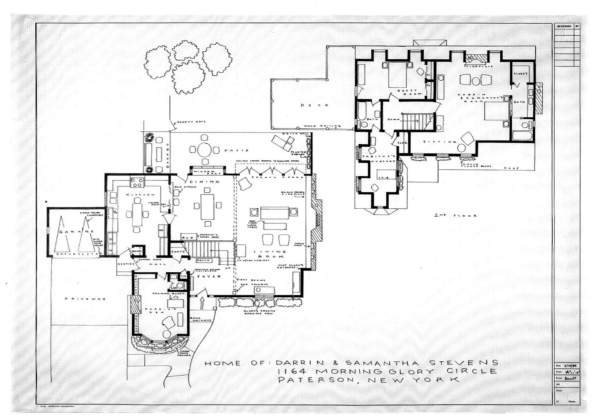

Home of Darrin and Samantha Stevens, 1986-96, ink and pencil on graph vellum, 61x91.4cm

Darrin and Samantha Stevens House *The Stevens's home, at 1164 Morning Glory Circle in Patterson, New York, is a quaint Dutch Colonial built in the early 1960s. From the first time Samantha and Eudora twitched their magical powers to produce plants and furniture, the Stevens's home has been a quality residence of good taste. A two-level home of brick and wood, this gabled, steep-roofed structure consists of open living and dining rooms surrounding a prominent staircase near the foyer. A raised brick hearth and fireplace is a focal point of the living room, as are the three sets of French doors leading to the patio at the back. The dining area features a bay window with built-in seat cushions, a louver-shuttered pass-through, a Grecian mural panel, and fully-stocked bar (Martinis are a speciality of the house). Through a double-swinging service door, a modern kitchen offers a washer and dryer, a dishwasher, a range and oven (for Baked Alaska), and a broom closet. A breakfast table and four chairs are at the centre of the room. A hallway leads from the foyer to a garden door; a service porch and garage are outside. Here Darrin and Samantha keep their late-model Chevrolets, inside an automatically opening garage. Darrin's den is behind the large bay window at the front of the house. A fireplace and bookshelves are against one wall, a couch and drawing board near the window. A small bathroom is near the door. Upstairs, there is a master suite, complete with bathroom, dressing area and cosy fireplace. Darrin and Samantha's bed rests under a shuttered window off the dressing room. Two low dormer windows offer a view outside. There is a another bedroom, used as a guest room for Darrin's parents when they visit, and eventually as Tabitha's nursery. In general, furnishings are high-end and modern: Jens Risom coffee table, a four-cushioned couch, a Hans Wenger papa bear chair with ottoman, mixed with provincial Windsor chairs. Decorator perfect.*

CENTRAL VALLEY
Miles Coolidge

UTA BARTH
PROJECT

Ground #2, *1992, colour photograph on panel, 76.2x68.6x5.1cm*

UNDOING SPACE

Soo Jin Kim

As seen from the window of an aeroplane or train, the landscape is blurred, abstract, from things coming into view too quickly. This is when I feel at home, when everything is indistinguishable from other places in my mind, before being located as Los Angeles, or London, or Lumpur. When the scenery is all three and more places, unidentified, dislocated, an imaginary (home)land. You can never go home again.

In his *Worlds in a Small Room*, the photographer Irving Penn assembled people from far-flung points of the world 'together', taking portraits with a neutral, generic tarp providing the background for them all. This background covered up landscape and specificity of place, obliterating distance and difference in exchange for a humanist universality. Penn gives us a look at the exotic. Uta Barth's *Ground* series takes a different approach. Rather than isolating the subject, she gives us both the background and the things we see every day that pass by unscrutinised – that is, the way we really see things, rather than what we cannot see, or want to see.

The series' colour photographs, mounted on wood panels, begin as portraits: shot straight on, focused, steady – traditional portrait techniques that ordinarily document and symbolise a person's position, their power. The difference is that these representations of persons, families and groups exist without their inclusion, only their absent presence. The subject in the foreground of the image is conceptually pulled away, leaving us with everything but – with whatever stands behind. What is left is a garden, a room, a window, a study, a seascape of focus in the background, the sharp focus gone, still searching for the lost subject. As in tourism leaflets, this reversal of the gaze offers the viewer an anticipated image, which speaks about you but carries another name – Tahiti, Geneva, New York.

The role of the subject shifts. The viewer becomes the subject of the photos and the subject of the work becomes seeing, or perception. Photography is startling not because it can produce a sharp picture but because it imitates vision. Barth's photos refuse a pure look at perception as an isolated phenomenological study, instead remaining in the act of perception, never free from the double-duty of seeing and interpreting. They remain engaged within the apparatus. What we are seeing is what we always see – bits of sky, a glimpse of the sea, a pathway, corners, curtains, books. What we are seeing is the eye attempting distinctions. The conceptual matrix of the series – the focus on the foregrounded subject and his/her/its subsequent removal – questions the construction of pictures, of photographic memory and picture-perfect images. The subject-turned-invisible inverts the hierarchy of compositional elements traditionally used to read images. The general now reads as primary, allowing the symbolic to have greater weight.

Regardless of knowledge of the conceptual basis of her project, Barth's photographs read as everyday spaces. Not exotic, not unimaginable or tricky. The any-space-ness of these places are made familiar by recalling other images that resemble them. Other rooms, other windows, other gardens. A photographic memory is more than attention to detail, but a recollection of a past scenario; a 'picture-perfect' image is a picture of other idealised pictures, made up of everything I could imagine and nothing I would not expect. It is easy to produce a narrative from these images but the narrative is never permanent or singular. Imagine an academic sitting in a study filled with walls of neatly-packed, hard-bound books; a lover standing in a garden where the sun shines brightly and a bush of flowers juts forward; a child smiling hugely by the sea; a friend on a dirt road finally out of the forest of trees behind her. The beauty of these images is not simply the composition or colour or quality of light but the subject and environment's constant indeterminacy. The academic as student, child, lover of books, blind; the study at once a library, bookseller, movie set. There is a freedom in a place having the potential to be more than one place, of being 'any-space-whatevers',[1] that is akin to the freedom of imagination. A seascape being either of/from San Pedro or Southampton is the triumph of temporal perspective. What remains fixed is the background: a sea, a road, a study. What remains is everything: assurance, versatility, flexibility. Without the confines of specifics – of a distinct person, of a particular family, of a specific group – we are left in a wide-open space where place is undone and narrative is untangled. 'It is a perfectly singular space, which has merely lost its homogeneity, that is, the principle of its metric relations or the connection of its own parts, so that the linkages can be made in an infinite number of ways. It is a space of virtual conjunction, grasped as pure locus of the possible. What in fact manifests the instability, the heterogeneity, the absence of link of such a space, is a richness in potentials or singularities which are, as it were, prior conditions of all actualisation, all determination.'[2] Uta Barth's *Ground* photographs begin as portraits but end as reflections; the construction of pictures of the world over mere representations of the world.

Notes

1 A space that is no longer a particular determined space. Coined by Pascal Augé and used by Gilles Deleuze in *Cinema 1: The Movement Image*, University of Minnesota Press, 1986.

2 *ibid*, p109.

Ground #44, *1994, colour photograph on panel, 100.3x122x5.1cm*

Ground #65, *1996, colour photograph on panel, 70.5x78.7x5.1cm*

Ground #73, *1996, colour photograph on panel, 38.7x38.7x5.1cm*

Ground #42, *1994, colour photograph on panel, 28.6x26.7x5.1cm*

Ground #66, *1996, colour photograph on panel, 49.5x53.3x5.1cm*

Ground #74, *1996, colour photograph on panel, 45.7x57.2x5.1cm*

Ground #70, *1996, colour photograph on panel, 41.3x38.7x5.1cm*

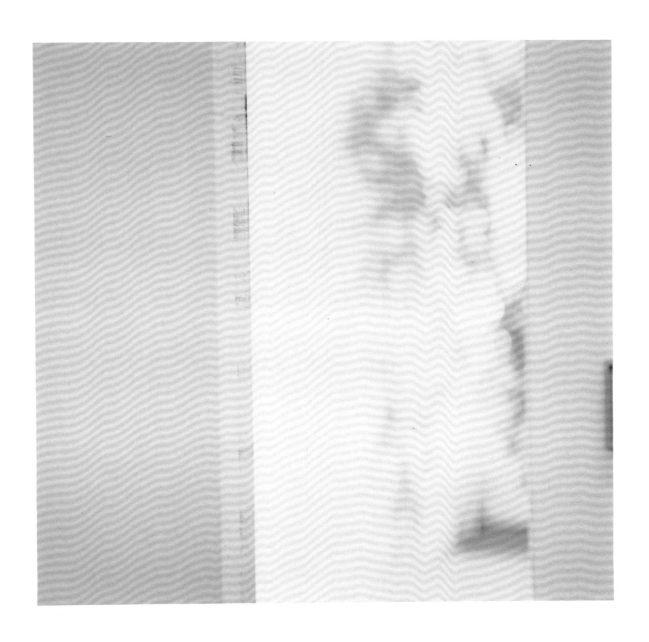

Ground #67, *1996, colour photograph on panel, 48.9x57.1x5.1cm*

FROM ABOVE: Kate Ericson and Mel Ziegler, Picture Out of Doors, *from the first 'Home Show', 1988, in which the artists removed all the doors within the occupant's home and stacked them in the living room. The inherent voyeurism of the show's concept was exacerbated by their insistent exposure of all the homeowner's belongings;* George Stone, Sinking Giant/Rising Shelter, *1996, 'Home Show 2'*

HOME SHOW 2
Michael Darling

Eight years ago, Santa Barbara, California, hosted the 'Home Show', a group exhibition that brought eleven contemporary artists into private homes for site-specific interventions. Sponsored by the Santa Barbara Contemporary Arts Forum (CAF), the show sought to expand the exhibition space beyond the confines of the publicly sanctioned white cube, and out into real, human space. Artists as far-ranging in their approaches as Ann Hamilton, Joseph Kosuth, Jim Isermann, Kate Ericson and Mel Ziegler decorated, transformed and deconstructed their respective sites in a manner that reflected both their own conceptual and aesthetic interests as well as the particularities of the homes and home owners themselves.

This year CAF debuted the sequel, 'Home Show 2' (April 20-June 2, 1996), in an effort to explore the artistic and social changes of the intervening years. As a member of the curatorial committee that brought together the current exhibition, I bring a certain insider's perspective to the discussion of the show that is predestined towards protective bias but which is not unaware of the shortcomings of some of the final results.

After roundtable discussions about the strengths and weaknesses of the first 'Home Show', including concerns about the showcase nature of many of the included houses and questions about the continued relevance of the notion of 'artistic intervention', the committee chose to direct the show towards a more focused exploration of the idea of 'home' in the mid-1990s. This would entail expanding the possible sites to include as many forms of 'home life' as possible. The end result is a collection of sites that ranges from a tony Montecito getaway to middle-class tract homes, a downtown retirement hotel, a trailer park, and a beach-side parking lot that is a frequent encampment for the homeless. A desire on the committee's part to represent a diverse cross-section of artistic activity matches the heterogeneity of the venues, where New Yorkers Vito Acconci, Dan Graham, Pepon Osorio and Allan Wexler are joined by the Chicago collaborative Haha, Seattle-based Buster Simpson, San Francisco collaborators Margaret Crane and Jon Winet, Los Angeles artists Linda Hudson and George Stone, and San Diego-based painter Jean Lowe.

Lowe's piece, *Decorating Hints*, is arguably the most entertaining work in the show, providing comic relief while interrogating the rampant tackiness and superficiality of popular culture. Adopting the cosy living and dining rooms of an historic 1920s-era Mediterranean house as her laboratory, Lowe concocts a makeshift library of painted papier-mâché books scat-

tered throughout the rooms. Mixed in and among the owner's existing book collection and various pieces of furniture – along with Lowe's own handmade, faux-woodgrain coffee table – are titillating tomes that take on religion, automobile culture, bird-watching, cooking and home security with a raucous fervour more germane to television talk shows. From 'The Ten Commandments: Are They Fair?' to 'Greener Pastures: Life After Marriage in Rural Idaho' and 'Jugs', a pictorial collection of lactating cows, Lowe's bizarre bibliography easily turns from funny to frightening when one realises that her subject matter is not very far away from the things discussed by Jerry Springer and Ricki Lake on TV, or in the supermarket tabloids. Lowe reveals the home as a creepy sanctuary for the consideration of popular conspiracy theories and oddball enthusiasms that bubble just beneath the mainstream of everyday discourse.

Dan Graham takes a more direct and unfiltered approach to a similar phenomenon in his *Video Projection Outside Home*. Here, Graham has simply placed a large screen television on the front lawn of a 1950s-era tract home, transmitting to the outside audience whatever programme is being watched inside by the house's occupants. This subtle shift from private consumption to public display turns a personal (and potentially incriminating) choice into a civic standard: when I stopped by, I got to watch a couple re-enact their vows of marriage, then slide into a pit of whipped cream and strip off their clothes (later, they won an all-expenses-paid trip to Orlando, Florida).

Elsewhere in the same neighbourhood, Vito Acconci performs a related inversion of standard conceptions of public and private space. In his *Talking House*, Acconci has wired an entire home for sound, transmitting idle chatter, bathroom noises and dinner-table discussions out onto the sidewalk for all to hear. Acconci's piece continues investigations with which the artist has been involved for the past 25 years; and when this house is brimming with activity (as is common in a busy family with two high-schoolers), it is equal to any of his better works.

One of the disappointments of the exhibition is an installation by Buster Simpson entitled *The Silver Anniversary of 'An American Family'*. As proposed, Simpson was to have made a contemporary update and retrospection on a now-infamous public-television experiment: the telecast of a Santa Barbara family's everyday activities. During the seven months in 1971 they were being filmed, the family disintegrated – and the debacle later broadcast for public consumption.

Somewhere between the proposal and its final installation,

'Home Show 2', FROM ABOVE, L TO R: Allan Wexler, Five Yardsaver Homes, *1996; Dan Graham*, Video Projection Outside Home, *1996; Jean Lowe*, Decorating Hints, detail, *1996; Pepon Osorio*, State of Preservation, *1996 (all photos in this essay by Wayne McCall)*

Simpson's generative concept broke down. As it was ultimately installed, the artist's piece resembled a domestic funeral pyre, with blackened television sets (playing edited footage of the 1971 programme) included among other household rubble, making little or no connection to either the site or the conceptual material.

There were a few other mild casualties along the risky route of speculative commissions, including George Stone's *Sinking Giant/Rising Shelter*, an open, tent-like structure based on the shape of Philadelphia's iconic Liberty Bell – here intended to serve as a temporary shelter for Santa Barbara's large homeless population. The metaphor of the bell is lost on many visitors, perhaps because of its self-obfuscating position, or its even more confusing patchwork covering (a suggestion of a monumental hobo perhaps?). Margaret Crane and Jon Winet's *Accommodations*, which was intended to transform a moderately derelict house-trailer into a high-tech information command centre, is uninspiring and rather ineffectual: a self-billed 'conduit to cyberspace' including two computer terminals, a string of black-and-white photographs ringing the trailer's walls, and an inexplicable, blue-lit meditation chamber in the bedroom.

An altogether more promising and pragmatic offering is Allan Wexler's *Five Yardsaver Homes*, an installation of five prefabricated metal storage sheds arranged to form a small neighbourhood of dwellings in a parking lot at Santa Barbara's East Beach. Wexler's units are variously equipped for use, some featuring inventive and multi-functional built-in furniture; one insulated for more demanding climes; and another outfitted with plywood wall cladding that might make a nice little art studio. Revisiting the postwar American passion for economical yet picture-perfect housing solutions, Wexler's 'homes' provide habitable, if not exactly luxurious, models for emergency shelter.

Pepon Osorio and Linda Hudson's installations offer architectural solutions of a more elective type, each serving as cultural/regional self-portraits in the process. Osorio's *State of Preservation* transplants the practice of slip-covering furniture in clear plastic (common in the artist's South Bronx neighbourhood) to a Montecito idyll that could be featured on the cover of *House Beautiful* – a sly conflation of socio-economic stereotypes that cuts to the persistent distance between the classes. Hudson's *Moving In*, on the other hand, plays on connections between homeowner and artist: Hudson expands upon the owner's future plans for converting an attic space into a bedroom. The proposed conversion, devised in collaboration with architect Wayne Schlock, is hinted at through blueprints, beautifully articulated translucent partition walls, and exterior screens of metal cable that fit right in with the material vocabulary of current Southern California architecture – as well as the adaptive approach followed by local luminaries Frank Gehry, Eric Owen Moss, and Franklin D Israel. Hudson and Schlock's work is one of the few projects that might be imagined as a permanent solution after the show is over.

The final piece, a collection of brief videos by Haha entitled *Hotel Shorts*, documents a living situation that was anything but permanent. *Hotel Shorts* started out as a film project intended to capture the personalities and perspectives of residents at a local low-cost residential hotel; but after filming was underway, it was discovered that the hotel would have to be closed and the residents displaced for a state-mandated structural retrofit. Follow-up interviews were conducted to glean the residents' reactions; the resulting footage makes for a heart-wrenching portrait of a community in flux. Haha's work, which was aired in the Contemporary Arts Forum's galleries and on a public access television station, provides a grounding in reality that binds the entire exhibition into a thought-provoking whole.

Hotel Shorts, along with the rest of the 'Home Show 2' projects (whether successful or not), fulfill the exhibition's goal of reorienting towards an exploration of the social, personal, and political realities of domestic shelter. The lasting impression of the show might, therefore, be characterised less as a collection of viscerally commanding artistic statements (the legacy of the first 'Home Show'), than as a lingering awareness of the interconnections between private and public life, and the boundaries that differentiate and divide individuals within those spheres. And unlike other exhibitions of provocative public art, these artists were able to engage the imagination of a community simply by staying firmly planted at home.

JUDY FISKIN

HOME

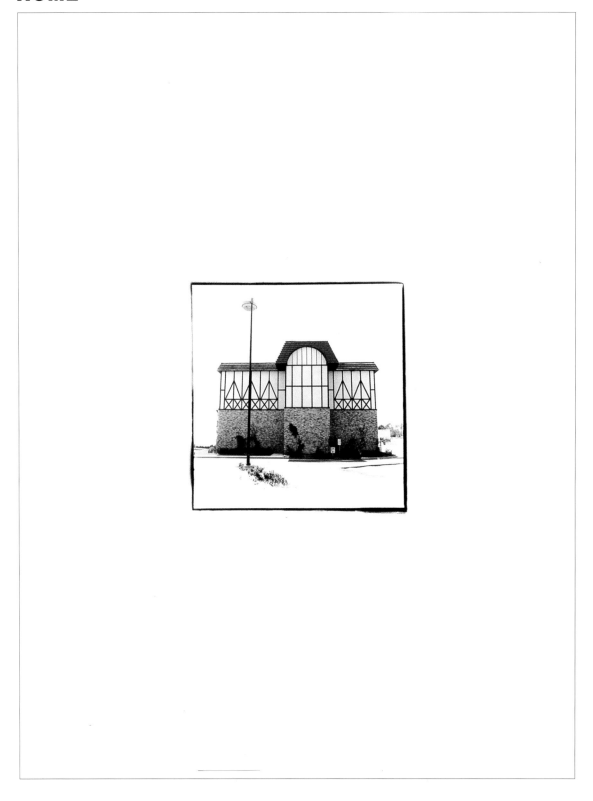

Portraits of Architecture, *1988, black and white photograph, 6x6cm*

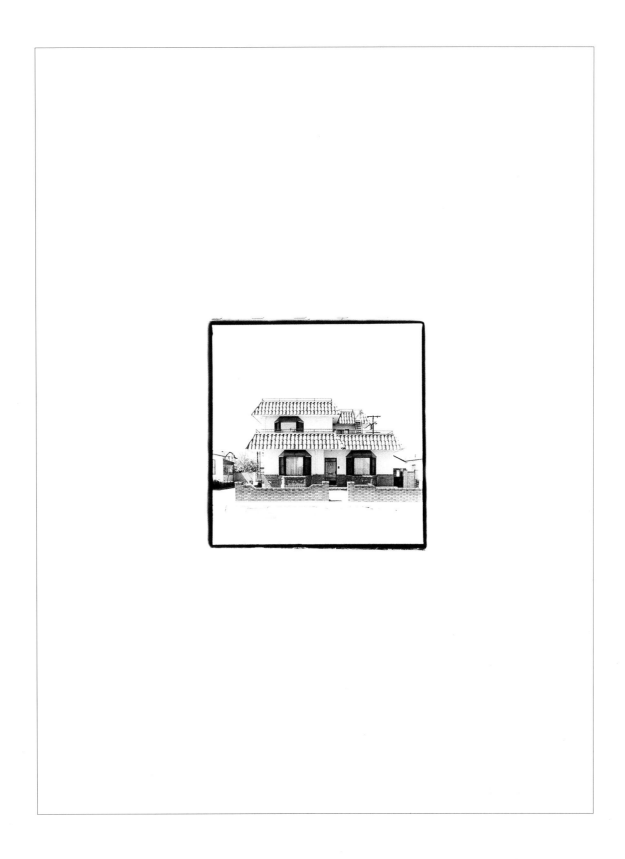

Portraits of Architecture, *1988, black and white photograph, 6x6cm*

Dingbat, *1982, black and white photograph, 6x6cm*

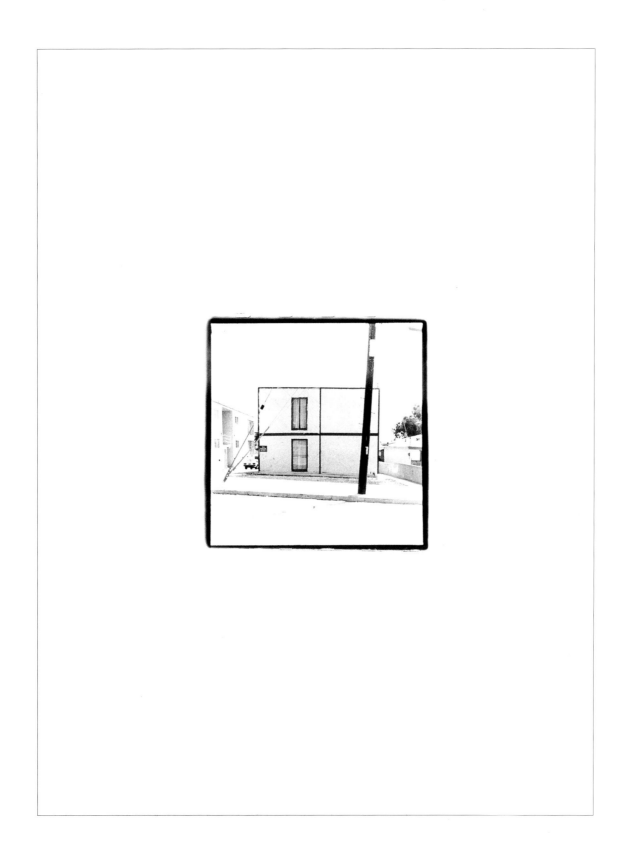

Portraits of Architecture, *1988, black and white photograph, 6x6cm*

DÉCOR

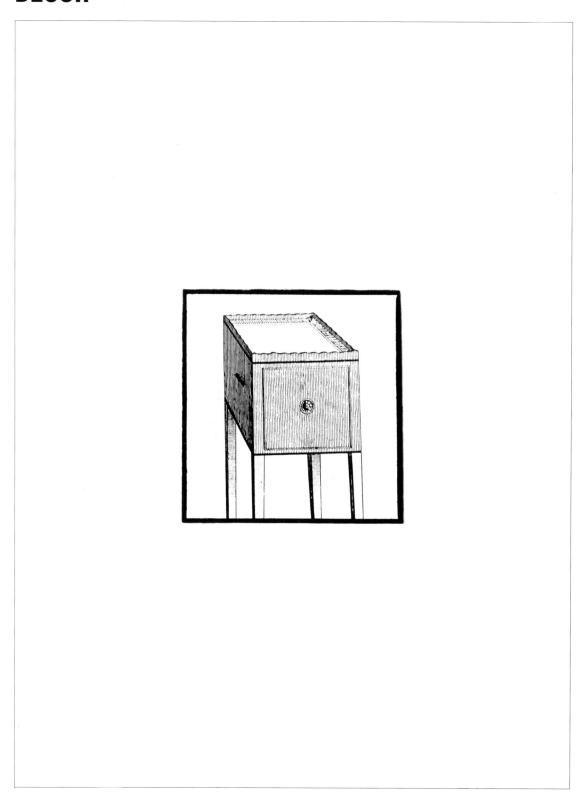

More Art, *1991, black and white photograph, Hepplewhite table, 6x6cm*

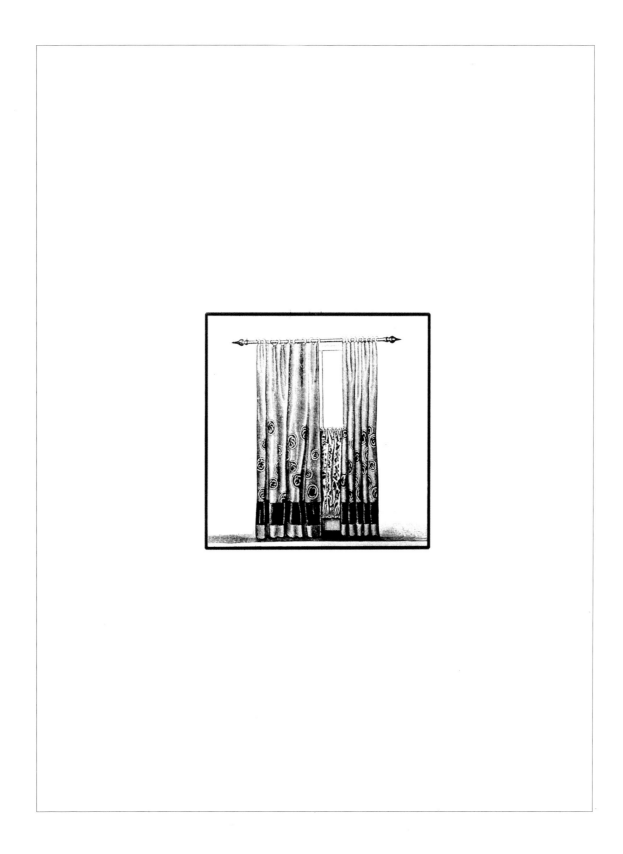

More Art, *1993, black and white photograph, 6x6cm*

Some Art, *1989, black and white photograph, anonymous painting, 6x6cm*

More Art, *1992, black and white photograph, 19th-century American embroidery, 6x6cm*

FROM ABOVE, L to R: Untitled (Woman Feeding Bird), *1990, silver print, 69.2x69.2cm;* Untitled (Nude), *1990, silver print, 69.2x69.2cm;* Untitled (Man Reading Newspaper), *1990, two of a triptych, silver prints, 69.2x69.2cm*

BY ANY MEANS NECESSARY
DOCUMENT AND FICTION IN THE WORK OF CARRIE MAE WEEMS
Lucy Soutter

The wooden rolling pin, a tool for making pastry, is also a potential weapon. As depicted in a large-format Polaroid photograph, with the caption 'By Any Means Necessary', the rolling pin evolves further: with it, the artist Carrie Mae Weems signals domesticity, women's work, anger, violence, revolutionary politics. This image is part of the installation 'And 22 Million Very Tired and Very Angry People' (1991), an encyclopaedic exploration of African-American identity, relationships and history as presented through photographs and a series of banners with text – including calls to action, awareness and unity by Malcolm X, Antonio Gramsci and Fanny Lou Hamer.

Like most of Weems's photographs, *By Any Means Necessary* can also circulate in isolation from its series, with its themes intact but its meanings looser and more indeterminate. Its caption evokes not only Malcolm X's slogan but also an artistic philosophy: the varying formal strategies Weems uses in her work are means to both artistic and political ends. By frequently changing her art's format and narrative structure, Weems thwarts assumptions of how political art should look and act. Rather than calcifying into a single mature style, her work continues to surprise and provoke, even as it gains critical and institutional recognition.

Some of Weems's photos are straightforward documents, some are staged fictional scenes and others are appropriated from historical sources. What binds them together, in Weems's eye, is their use as story elements that articulate lived experience. Of her installation 'Family Pictures and Stories', (1978-84) Weems has said: 'There are some photographs in this room that stand on their own as just lovely pictures, some of them are okay photographs, and some are mediocre – you can get along without them. But the ones that really interest me the most, regardless of their beauty as objects, are those which have the wonder, the texture and the precision of the language that rests beneath them.'[1]

While she shares certain strategies with contemporary photo-artists like Jeff Wall, Cindy Sherman or Barbara Kruger – playing with representational tropes from painting, cinema and advertising – Weems's practice is more firmly rooted in photographic tradition, specifically that of social documentary. This is especially evident in her first series, which grew out of the political activism in which she was involved in the late 1970s. Entitled 'Environmental Portraits', the series is composed of images of the African-American community in San Francisco, drawing upon the tradition of the photo-essay, a form in which photographs and social narrative work together. Her later multi-layered constructions of photographs and text recall such precedents as Langston Hughes and Roy De Carava's *Sweet Flypaper of Life* (1955), a lyrical document of life in Harlem; Richard Wright's *12 Million Black Voices* (1941), a text accompanying photographs selected from the Farm Securities Administration (FSA) project; and James Agee and Walker Evans's *Let Us Now Praise Famous Men* (1941), an anti-narrative which struggles to represent disenfranchised tenant farmers.

In keeping with these models, Weems tackles large-scale institutional problems by mapping them onto personal spaces. Often, these spaces are her own: In *Family Pictures and Stories*, (1978-84), she takes her audience on a trip to her childhood home in Oregon. Snapshots, anecdotal captions and an audiotape of stories and interviews combine to create a nuanced and ambivalent document. Weems created the series, in part, as a response to the Moynihan Report (entitled 'The Negro Family: The Case for National Action'), a demographic study commissioned by the US government in 1965.[2] Weems's work provides a counterpoint to the way in which the study tore specific problems from their social context. Weems acts as social historian, anthropologist, ethnographer and folklorist. Teenage pregnancy, violence between father and son and marital infidelity are revealed not as racially inherent ills, but as complex layers in a multi-generational saga of survival. While the *Family Pictures and Stories* photographs alone might trigger a voyeuristic response, Weems's attendant narratives invite a kind of imaginative identification.

In traditional social documentary, a certain degree of subjectivity has always been seen as necessary, even desirable; though the intentional manipulation or construction of fact is taboo. Yet as social documentary has become institutionalised in the popular press and in museums during the latter half of the 20th century, the persistent tendency of the camera to turn its subject into a mythical 'other' (no matter who is behind the lens) has become a troubling critical dilemma. Socially committed photographers have hence searched for strategies to sidestep this liability.[3] Weems turns, radically, to fiction.

Weems combines the social concerns of documentary with the empathic potential of fiction. Her *Untitled* ('Kitchen Table Series') (1990) is a novelistic construction of imaginary, though semi-autobiographical, events. With characters, plot and a rich material culture of costumes and props, the series is structured as a *bildungsroman* – a story in which a character

Untitled (Eating Lobster), *1990, silver print, 69.2x69.2cm*

She felt monogamy had a place but invested it with little value. It was a system, based on private property, an order defying human nature. Personally she wasn't in the mood for exploring new rocky terrain. But nonetheless assured him she was secure enough in herself and their love to allow him space to taste the exotic fruits produced in such abundance by mother nature.

He was grateful for such generosity. He certainly knew the breadth of his own nature, so felt human nature was often in need of social control. For now he chose self-sacrifice for the long term benefits of her love and their relationship. Testing the strength of the relationship in this way was a dangerous game; taking a chance now might be more than either of them bargained for.

Untitled (Woman Standing Alone), *1990, silver print, 69.2x69.2cm each*

She was working, making long money, becoming what he called 'bourgie', he wasn't working and this was truly messing with his mind. He was starting to feel like a Black man wasn't supposed to have nothing, like some kind of conspiracy was being played out and he was the fall guy, like the mission was impossible, like it ain't a man's world, like just cause she was working and making so much dough, she was getting to where she didn't love him no mo, like he had bad luck, like he didn't have a dream, like he needed a night in Tunisia, like he needed to catch a freight train and ride, like if he felt tomorrow like he did today, come Sunday he'd pack up and sure make a get-away, like if he stayed, the kid would hate him for sure, like he just might have to contribute to the most confusing day in Harlem, like he had a tomb-stone disposition and a grave-yard mind. Like maybe a Black man just wasn't her kind.

grows into mature identity through a series of trials. While the overarching narrative frame may be familiar to Western high culture, the specific content is not: Weems herself models as a black woman who takes a lover, has a child, earns professional success, loses the lover, takes comfort in friends and ultimately finds completion in herself.

Fiction has a history of providing space for marginalised people to imagine themselves in new ways.[4] It can provoke an identification and self-recognition that leads to changed perception. Of course, not all forms of fiction are productive, some offer sheer escapism. In her work, Weems is not opposed to such pleasurable escape: Love, described in Weems's work as 'that ol' black magic', has qualities of illusion and delusion that her characters embrace willingly, knowing that they risk disappointment. The text panels that accompany her photographs are often woven from familiar blues lyrics and well-worn clichés. Yet these comfortable words do not cover up pain but make it possible for it to be more fully expressed and endured.

The characters' difficulties are most acute where their lives intersect with received cultural roles. For example, in the 'Kitchen Table Series', Weems addresses the stereotype of the black matriarchal family: the woman as too successful, the man as not successful enough: 'She was working, making long money, becoming what he called "bourgie", he wasn't working and this was truly messing with his mind.' Unlike Cindy Sherman, whose staged self-portraits self-consciously reiterate two-dimensional stereotypes, Weems takes an active part in constructing new visual roles for her characters, connecting them in a complex social web. The photographs of the female character in the 'Kitchen Table Series' as lover, mother and friend provide vital context for the images in which she is alone.

The power that Weems claims for her character is most evident in the images in which her central activity is posing. In *Untitled (Nude)* she is naked, flaunting her beauty in an extraordinarily uninhibited way, using her body to confront the paucity of black female nudes in the history of art by African-Americans.[5] In *Untitled (Woman Standing Alone)* she is isolated at the centre of the frame, meeting the viewer's gaze with complete self-possession. The kitchen, long considered a trap for women, becomes a setting for personal discovery.

Weems's *Untitled* ('Sea Islands Series') (1991-92) also incorporates aspects of documentary and fiction, but with different formal means. Instead of centring a narrative around a single family or character, Weems uses domestic spaces and objects as elements of a broader cultural archaeology. Travelling to the isolated Gullah Islands of Georgia and South Carolina (a point of entry for 18th-century slaves, whose descendants still reside there), she collected visual and linguistic traces of lost African culture. Her findings take many forms: the installation includes original photographs; appropriated daguerreotypes; panels printed with myths, folk wisdom, and songs; and memorial ceramic plates with texts that begin with the formula, 'Went Looking for Africa and Found. . .' Weems also sets up photographs of interior spaces to illustrate the superstitions and rituals which African-Americans have used to protect themselves from evil: a hat lying on a bed foreshadows disaster; an empty chair stands beside a bowl of water, while a text panel provides an interpretation: 'If a person comes to your home and you sense bad karma, put out a pan of water and when the person leaves, take it outside and dump it.'

These unoccupied interiors have an earnest elegance, reminiscent of Walker Evans' images of sharecropper's homes. However, Evans was engaged in an act of reverent violation, imposing an aesthetic of stark beauty in an attempt to document a world that was not his. Weems counters Evans's inadvertent fiction-making with deliberate fictions of her own. Realising that traditional social documentary is, and has been, inadequate to capture lived experience, Weems employs fiction as a powerful aid to creative and cultural survival. Imagination and documentation are equally valued in reconstructing fragments that have been broken, lost or neglected.

Notes

1 Lois Tarlow, 'Carrie Mae Weems', *Art New England 12* (August/September 1991), p11.

2 Andrea Kirsh, 'Carrie Mae Weems: Issues in Black, White and Color', *Carrie Mae Weems* (Washington, DC: The National Museum of Women in the Arts, 1994), p11.

3 Women, for example, used novels to educate themselves before they had access to higher education. Raymond Williams describes the way in which 19th-century British women, eager to discuss what they had read, were the catalyst for the formation of the academic study of English Literature, 'The Future of Cultural Studies', *The Politics of Modernism: Against the New Conformists*, Verso, London, 1994, p152.

4 A valuable discussion of this issue is provided by Martha Rosler, 'In Around and Afterthoughts (on Documentary Photography)', *The Contest of Meaning*, Richard Bolton, ed, The MIT Press, Cambridge, 1989.

5 Judith Wilson addressed this representational problem in a discussion of contemporary culture at the Dia Center for the Arts: 'Getting Down to Get Over: Romare Bearden's Use of Pornography and the Problem of the Black Female Body in Afro-US Art', *Black Popular Culture, A Project by Michele Wallace*, Bay Press, Seattle, 1992.

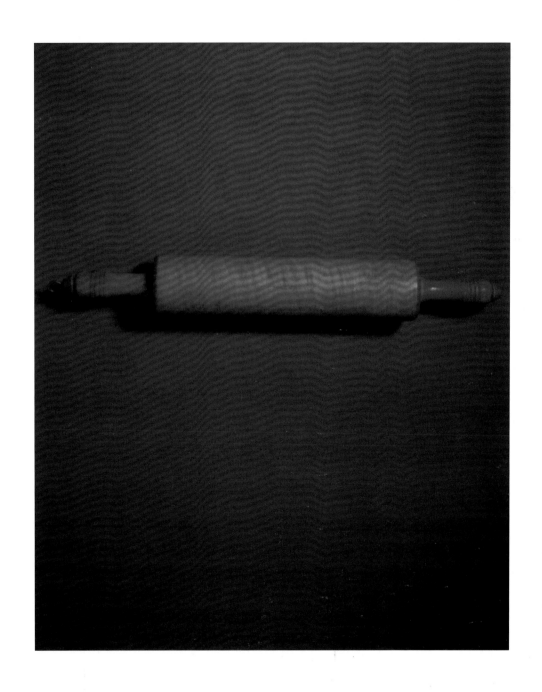

By Any Means Necessary, *1991, Polaroid colour print, 60.9x50.8cm*

Florine Stettheimer, Portrait of My Sister Carrie with Dollhouse, *1923, oil on canvas*

THE HOUSE THAT CARRIE BUILT
THE STETTHEIMER DOLL'S HOUSE OF THE 1920s
Janine Mileaf

Lots of little girls furnish doll's houses. Some even customise the interiors to suit the needs of imaginary inhabitants. However, few of these treasured objects enter the hallowed halls of museums. Those that do are often the playthings of the rich or famous: Queen Mary, for example, or Carole and Barry Kaye, whose private museum in Los Angeles houses an opulent doll's house collection. Carrie Stettheimer's doll's house, which has been on permanent display at the Museum of the City of New York since 1945, is no exception.[1] Its celebrated art gallery, working elevator and 1920s panache reflect the social milieu of its maker, who along with her sisters Florine and Ettie, hosted an avant-garde salon in New York during the inter-war years.[2]

Tucked away in the museum's toy collection, the Stettheimer doll's house has been a pilgrimage site for families whose daughters (and occasionally, sons) have shared Carrie's obsession. Lately, however, a new breed of spectator has taken an interest in the Stettheimer doll's house. It has been used as the location for a fashion spread in the *New York Times Magazine* (accomplished through computer imaging),[3] and was featured in an exhibition at the Smithsonian Institution's National Portrait Gallery in Washington, DC.[4]

More significantly, doll's houses like the Stettheimer one, have recently gained new stature among fine-art audiences. Doll's houses, with their connotations of the domestic, the feminine and the childlike, are hardly the stuff of which 20th-century art history is made. However, now that there is a renewed scholarly interest in Feminist art of the 1970s, and its echoes are being seen in the work of contemporary artists such as Laurie Simmons and Charles LeDray (who have turned towards such subjects and techniques as the family and knitting), the doll's house is experiencing a renaissance.

Carrie Stettheimer benefits from this revision along with her sister Florine, a painter whose eclectic, campy tableaux were resurrected in a recent retrospective at the Whitney Museum of American Art in New York,[5] and in a biography by Barbara J Bloemink.[6] Neglected during the reign of masculine, heroic painting of the 1950s up through the ironic, appropriative vocabularies of the last decade, Florine Stettheimer's work has re-emerged as contemporary painting which too, turns its attention to the decorative and domestic.[7]

The Stettheimers were an unconventional family unit: three women in their 40s – Carrie, Florine, and Ettie – and their ageing mother, Rosetta. The four women settled in New York's Upper West Side in 1914, after more than a decade of European travel that began when Joseph Stettheimer, a banker of German-Jewish origin, abandoned his wife and children, and ended with the outbreak of World War I. Two older children, Walter and Stella, had earlier married and moved to California, but the remaining Stettheimer sisters stayed with their mother until her death in 1935.

In the resulting all-female ménage, each sister forged an individual identity and vocation. Ettie, who received a doctoral degree in philosophy from the University of Freiburg, Germany, was the flirtatious wit who published novels under the pseudonym Henrie Waste (from her full name Henrietta Walter Stettheimer). Florine, the artist, was the introvert who avoided public exhibitions but chronicled the family's interactions in flamboyant and revealing paintings. Carrie, strongly associated with the home in her creative pursuits, also played the domestic doyenne in everyday life. As the eldest of the sisters, she took on many of the household duties, including entertaining the demi-monde and caring for Rosetta in her old age.

Carrie Stettheimer's decorative style, with its flamboyant pinks and acid greens, floral patterns and reflective surfaces was considered ahead of its time by early commentators.[8] Her doll's house, custom-built *c*1917 to her specifications, has 17 rooms, each in its own motif. The facade is neoclassical, with two-storey columns flanking the doors. There are Venetian and Victorian bedrooms, a library with Chinese-inspired décor, an Empire foyer and landing, and a brightly coloured nursery with *papier coupé* Noah's Ark frieze. The doll's house is decorated largely with store-bought furnishings that Carrie customised to suit each room's design: hand-made needlepoint and velvet carpets; fabric, lace, and paper wall coverings; painted furniture. A *vue d'optique* of French gardens exaggerates the sense of perspective on the upstairs landing, to which the elevator ascends. The house's library holdings include titles by the Stettheimers' writer friends; monogrammed handkerchiefs arranged on the dressing table in the master bedroom further particularise the space.

The mannequins of avant-garde characters that now people the doll's house were not of Carrie's creation. They were added in 1976 by John Noble, former Curator of the Toy Collection at the Museum of the City of New York, when the house underwent refurbishing.[9] While not original, these figures, based on Florine's paintings, bring the Stettheimer's family life and social interactions into focus.

The most acclaimed aspect of the house is the ballroom, which boasts original miniatures by the Stettheimers' friends Marcel Duchamp, Albert Gleizes, Gala and Alexander Archipenko, Marguerite and William Zorach, and Gaston Lachaise, among others. In a small way, Carrie Stettheimer became a premier collector of avant-garde art: Duchamp's tiny *Nude Descending A Staircase* was a gift to Carrie on her birthday in 1918.[10] In the 1940s, Duchamp again reproduced his celebrated painting in miniature, this time for inclusion in a portable museum entitled *Boîte-en-valise*. This leather-bound suitcase contained 69 reproductions of Duchamp's works, including three-dimensional models of famous readymades like *Fountain*, 1917, and *Air de Paris*, 1919. Given the similarities in scale between the doll's house and the suitcase – and the related process of reproduction enacted in each – it is not unrealistic to suggest that Carrie's art gallery served as a precedent for Duchamp's travelling retrospective.

Carrie left few written records, so what is known of her history largely derives from Ettie's words and Florine's pictures. In the foreword to the catalogue that was published after Carrie's death and upon donation of the doll's house to the museum, Ettie noted that although an extremely competent housekeeper, Carrie 'had no liking whatever for this job'.[11] Although Ettie worked to disassociate her late sister from the domestic sphere, Carrie herself had already defied traditional stereotypes of women in the home by assuming her responsibilities with flair. She was known for wild party menus – oyster salad and feather soup – and haute couture.

The parallelism of Carrie's tendency towards self-adornment and her interest in the doll's house was not missed by Florine, who painted her sister's portrait in 1923. Here, Florine figures Carrie as the stylish proprietress of overlapping realms of existence. With the doll's house as her identifying attribute, Carrie stands in their apartment before an expansive outdoor scene. She is hostess of the manor as well as sovereign of the miniature. 'Decorator, Designer & Collector', Florine declared in the painting, as if it were inscribed on a bronze plaque affixed to the doll's house.

This portrait constructs a wonderfully complex identity for Carrie in a conflation of interior and exterior, imagination and reality. Florine serialises time through multiple representations of Carrie and collapses spatial relationships by dissolving the walls of their New York apartment. In a white evening dress, cloche hat with antennae-like protrusions, jewelled choker and earrings, lace shawl and black, fur-lined train, Carrie points to the doll's house with one hand while inserting an upholstered chair through the front door. The white and black-accented palette of Carrie's clothing is duplicated in the doll's house's facade, thus merging the identities of each.

Carrie stands on a pale blue carpet that is flowered and monogrammed with the initials 'CS'. The plane of the floor tilts upwards so that this carpet, rather than any architectural detail, delineates a window ledge. Beyond the window, the Stettheimer family lunches in a scene reminiscent of another of Florine's paintings, *Family Portrait #1*, 1915. The repetition of an earlier composition here functions as a memory, while further explicating familial interactions. The image of the family, including a rare depiction of the Stettheimers' brother Walter, might be an image in Carrie's mind, but it also refers to Florine's art. It is not framed as a picture within a picture, but as a real – or remembered – event. Beyond the luncheon fare, a farm scene with tractor, cow and ploughed fields completes Carrie's dominion, suggesting that her imagined and actual households extend beyond the boundaries of the miniature world she creates in the doll's house.

Unmarried, childless women were held in suspicion by the mainstream in Carrie's day. Because of the exclusively female nature of the Stettheimer enclave and the fact that none of the sisters ever married, Carrie's doll's house has been suggested as a surrogate for a 'normal' family structure. Commentators often see the doll's house as an opportunity for Carrie to establish a home 'of her own',[12] since she lived with her mother for most of her adult life. However, it can be argued that on the contrary, Carrie's attraction to the doll's house stemmed from the very fact that it was unreal, and did not require the kind of labour associated with running a family. It may have signified a realm of play and fantasy, detached from the drudgery and responsibility with which Carrie was quite familiar as the sister charged with most of the familial duties.

Despite such appealing interpretations, even Ettie described the doll's house as a substitution of a sort. When writing about Carrie's aspirations in the 1947 catalogue, Ettie identified a lack in terms of profession, rather than progeny:

> I am tempted to confide to all interested that I look upon this production of Carrie's as a facile and more or less posthumous substitute for the work she was eminently fitted to adopt as a vocation, had the circumstances been favourable: stage design.[13]

Note that Ettie did not propose the more obvious *métier* of interior design for her sister, but rather turned towards the public arena of the theatre. The affinity between doll's house-decorating and interior design must surely have been apparent to Carrie and her sisters; however, this newly professionalised field quickly acquired negative – ie, gendered – connotations that Ettie wanted to avoid when establishing her sister's legacy. This bias against female designers as spinsters, or even lesbians, was made apparent in the popular press: *Vogue* magazine related the commonly-held belief in a 1921 issue, observing, 'Someone once said that a woman is either happily married or an Interior Decorator.'[14] Given such aspersions, it is not surprising that in her final tribute to Carrie's creativity, Ettie allied her sister's activities with the stage, not the home.

Carrie probably did not consider her doll's house in terms of Modern art, either. Decorated in the trendiest styles of the day, the house, like Carrie herself, set the pace of fashion in the 1920s – but did not press beyond the domestic into the masculinised spheres of art. During those early years of the American avant-garde, painting was beginning to be associated with abstraction, purity and universal form. The decorative, considered frivolous and feminised, was ultimately banished from such lofty realms.[15] Nonetheless, Carrie's lifestyle and artistic affiliations were on the cutting edge of bohemia.

The doll's house may be more closely linked to the experimental art practices of such Stettheimer friends as Marcel Duchamp than has previously been considered: Duchamp's notions of replication and readymade, which were played out in the *Boîte-en-valise*, suggest that art is not found in expressive, individualistic formats but in the artist's process of selection. Store-bought, manufactured and gathered by an iconoclast, Duchamp's objects were understood as brilliantly subversive; assembled in a doll's house and in a domestic setting, Carrie's related wares could not be seen as the same.

Although Carrie's doll's house was never promoted as carrying within it the ironic detachment or self-conscious wit of Duchamp or his conceptual descendants, formally it fits within a trajectory of alternative techniques that have been celebrated as antidotes to abstraction throughout the 20th century: Carrie's activities of sewing, embroidering, shopping, gluing and arranging have become familiar in assemblages by Surrealist and Pop artists, and in postmodern works by appropriationists from Haim Steinbach to Sylvie Fleury.

Furthermore, the doll's house shares its focus on the

FROM ABOVE: Florine, Carrie and Ettie (left to right) Stettheimer, c 1914, photo-montage on postcard, whereabouts unknown; Carrie Walter Stettheimer's doll's house with facade raised to show front rooms, c 1916-35; Carrie Walter Stettheimer's doll's house, detail of ballroom

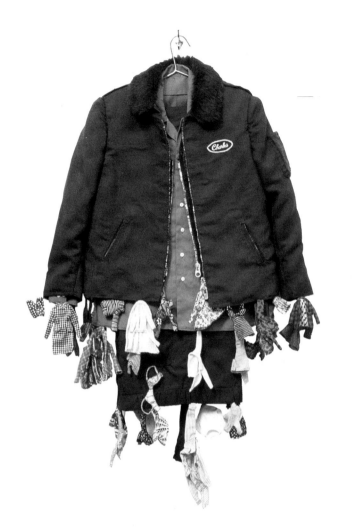

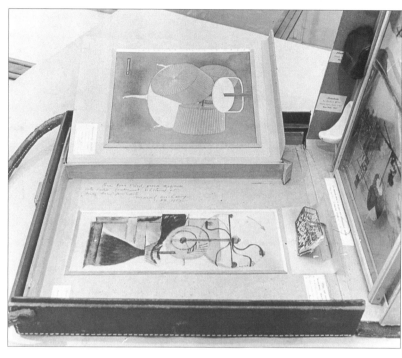

FROM ABOVE, L to R: Charles LeDray, Charles, *1995*; Marcel Duchamp, Boîte-en-valise (Box in a Valise), *1941*; Mme Albert Gleizes powders her nose in the master bedroom (photo David Levinthal, 1995); Baroness de Meyer (left) chats with Carrie Stettheimer in the foyer, while Pavel Tchelitchew rides in the elevator (photo David Levinthal, 1995)

domestic – or the escape from same – with a variety of more politically oppositional artists. Perceived as outside dominant artistic vocabularies, the home has been a site for polemical works of art since the 1970s, when Feminist artists began to reclaim such gendered spaces. 'Womanhouse', 1971-72, a collaborative project in which 23 female artists took over a dilapidated Los Angeles mansion to reinvent its interior, employed the imaginative activity of decoration to make ideological assertions.[16] This life-sized house included such memorable rooms as Judy Chicago's *Menstruation Bathroom*, in which hundreds of store-bought sanitary supplies were arranged on a bathroom shelf and in an overflowing wastebasket in the centre of the floor. While neglected by some mainstream art historians in the decades since its production, 'Womanhouse' is now receiving renewed attention as the strategies developed there have become of interest to contemporary artists, and its artist-members canonised in institutional histories of Feminist art.

While the echoes of experimental 1970s critiques can be seen in the more ideologically focused, large-scale domestic installations of Ann Hamilton and many others, interest in the home has not been restricted to Feminist, or even female artists. In *Time Flies*, 1993, Stuart Netsky produced a latex-laden interior at the Institute of Contemporary Art in Philadel-phia to speak about gay domesticity; and exhibitions such as *Guys Who Sew*[17] have focused on Feminist art's formal and conceptual influence on contemporary male artists such as Mike Kelley and Robert Gober.

The Stettheimer doll's house subject and technique have each been recouped as the canon of art has been reformatted. No longer confined within the folk tradition of toy-making, or even the history of leisure activities for the wealthy, the doll's house may be considered alongside assemblage, appropriation and installation art. Formerly acclaimed as a showplace for miniature modernist works of art, the Stettheimer doll's house itself may claim conceptual relevance as a site of aesthetisised resistance. To deny its significance because of Carrie's non-artist status, her identity as 'spinster', 'clothes-horse', or even 'housekeeper', is to restrict history to the level of individual experience.

Carrie Stettheimer embodied the modern in both her creative and social lives. In the doll's house, she mediated between the domestic and the artistic in an era that understood the two to be incompatible. By claiming and embellishing the feminised space of the home, the Stettheimer doll's house provides a miniature model for alternative art practices throughout the 20th century.

Notes

1 With thanks to Sheila Clark, Toy Collection Coordinator, Museum of the City of New York, for her generosity in sharing the Stettheimer archives with me, October 1994; and to Elizabeth Johns, Silfen Professor, University of Pennsylvania, in whose seminar I first considered the Stettheimer doll's house.

2 For more information regarding the Stettheimers' cultural era, see Stephen Watson, *Strange Bedfellows*, Abbeville Press, New York, 1991.

3 Jean Nathan with photographs by David Levinthal, 'Doll House Party', *New York Times Magazine*, July 16, 1995, pp36-41.

4 *Group Portrait: The First American Avant-Garde*, National Portrait Gallery, Smithsonian Institution, Washington, DC, May 10 – November 3, 1991.

5 *Florine Stettheimer: Manhattan Fantastica*, organised by Elisabeth Sussman and Barbara J Bloemink, was held at the Whitney Museum of American Art from July 13 – November 5, 1995, catalogue Harry N Abrams, New York, 1995.

6 Barbara J Bloemink, *The Life and Art of Florine Stettheimer*, Yale University Press, New York, 1995.

7 One early exception was an article written by feminist art historian Linda Nochlin, 'Florine Stettheimer: Rococo Subversive', *Art in America 68*, September 1980, pp64-83 and reprinted in the Whitney catalogue.

8 See Janet Pinney in *The Stettheimer Doll's House*, Museum of the City of New York, New York, 1947.

9 For more information on the renovation of the house, see John Noble, *A Fabulous Doll House of the Twenties*, Dover Publications, New York, 1976.

10 'Nu Descendent un Escalier ébuit pour la collection de la poupée de Carrie Stettheimer et a l'occasion de sa fête en bon souvenir Marcel Duchamp, 23 Juillet, New York', Stettheimer archives, Museum of the City of New York.

11 *The Stettheimer Doll's House*, Museum of the City of New York, New York, 1947, p4.

12 John Richardson, 'High Life in the Doll's House', *Vanity Fair*, December 1986, p110.

13 *The Stettheimer Doll's House*, Museum of the City of New York, New York, 1947, p4.

14 Quoted in Peter McNeil, 'Designing Women: Gender, Sexuality and the Interior Designer, c1890-1940', *Art History 17:4*, December 1994, p634.

15 A new anthology edited by Christopher Reed explores the incompatibility of domesticity and modernity. *Not At Home: The Suppression of Domesticity in Modern Art and Architecture*, Christopher Reed (ed), Thames and Hudson, London, 1996.

16 With thanks to Christopher Reed for bringing this connection to my attention.

17 October 5 – December 11, 1994, University Art Museum, University of California, Santa Barbara.

JIM ISERMANN

1

2

3

4

5

6

Photo Identification 1-6 Project Unité, 1993, fabric, linoleum, installation in Le Corbusier's Unité d'Habitation, Firminy-Vert, France; *7-8* TV Lounge, 1988, cowhide, vinyl, linoleum, acrylic yarn, enamel paint, wood, permanent installation at the American Museum of the Moving Image, Astoria, New York; *9-10* Futura, 1987, vinyl, carpet, enamel paint, wood, installation at the Los Angeles County Museum of Art; *11-12* TV Room, 1986 (destroyed 1994), vinyl, carpet, enamel paint, wood, video screening room for Los Angeles Contemporary Exhibitions; *13-14* Flowers, 1985, nylon webbing, enamel paint, wood, found lamps; *15* Suburban, 1984, vinyl, enamel paint, wood, found lamps; *16* Look Forward to Tomorrow, 1983, nylon webbing, plexiglas, enamel paint, wood, found objects; *17-18* Motel Modern, 1982, fake fur, enamel paint, wood, found lamps, installation at the Inn of Tomorrow, Anaheim, CA; *19* (0691), 1991, stained glass, 14.2x14.2cm; *20* (0492), 1992, stained glass, 14.2x14.2cm; *21* (0593), 1993, hand-pieced fabric, 75.6x75.6cm; *22* (0793), 1993, hand-pieced fabric, 75.6x75.6cm; *23* (0495), 1995, hand-loomed cotton, 20.5x19.7cm; *24* (1195), 1995, hand-loomed cotton and linen, 20.5x20.5cm. *Photo Credits: 9-16 Anthony Cunha, 17-18 Sheree Rose, 19-20 David Familian, 21-22 Peter Muscato, 23-24 Fredrik Nilsen.*

7

11

15

8

12

16

9

13

17

10

14

18

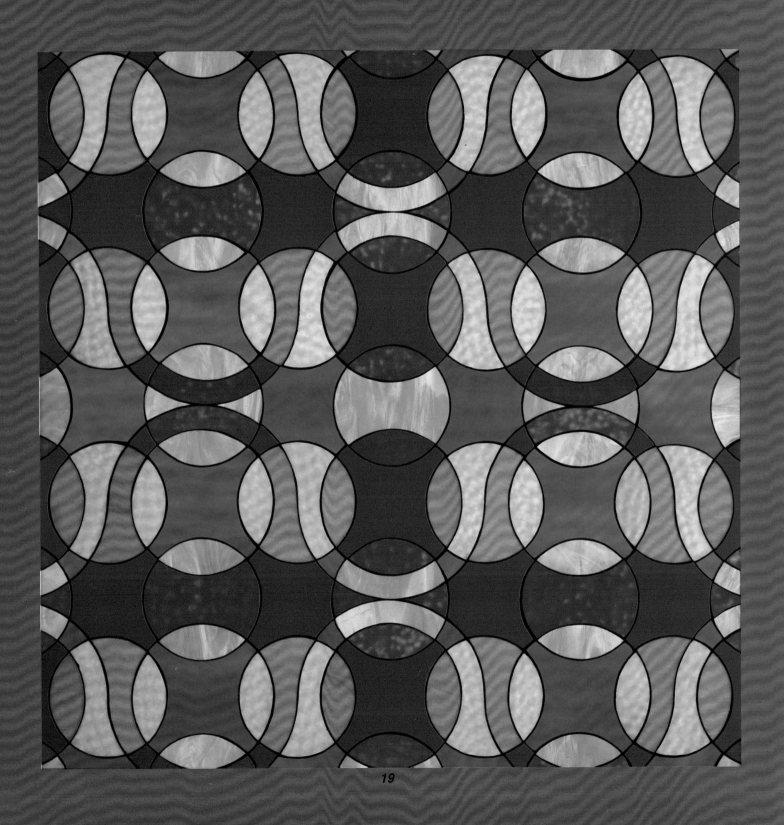

19

20

21

22

23

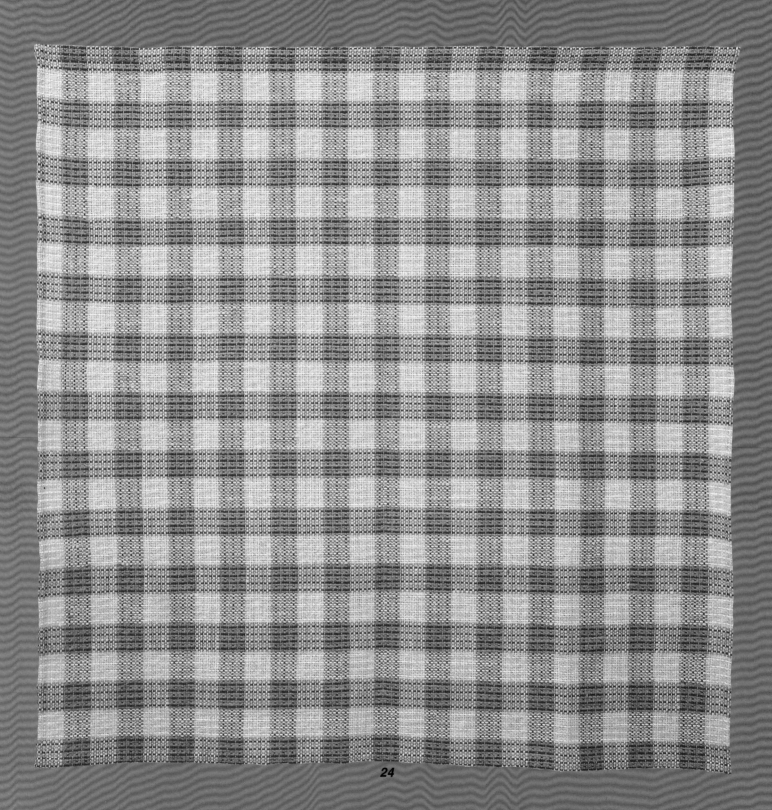

24

HOME
David A Greene

'Home' is one of those words that advertising copywriters adore, employing it to promote a vast, warm blanket of material accoutrements, all designed to transmogrify a box of wood/ steel/cement/cardboard/dirt/ice into neither a specific thing nor place, but an idea: a repository of memories, a forum for myth-making, a zone of comfort and safety. Snobs like the word, too, if for no other reason than to mock those who use it to excess, the ones who seek that elusive idea (or attempt to forestall its departure) through their purchases or other un- seemly pursuits – like genealogy-digging on the Internet or over-decorating at Christmas time or getting pregnant. But those who boast they do not need it invariably already have it; and all of us, when we discover it lacking, will search for it to the ends of the earth.

Or at least as far as Los Angeles. Many of the artists and writers in this edition of *Art & Design* currently live or have lived in LA; this is not an editorial plot. But if New York is the place we go when we know exactly what we want, then Los Angeles is the city we are drawn to when we wish to discover just what that might be. Hollywood clichés aside, LA is a vast basin of infinite choice, impossibly diverse in its peoples, land- scape, socio-economic and ideological strata. To forge a home there – a community of two or 2,000 – is a triumph of effort and will; it is also an exercise that will cause many to subsequently up and leave town. For to succeed is to realise that there are places elsewhere in the world far more hospitable to one's hard-won sense of home, and to its maintenance.

Some stay, of course. Indeed, some are even born and raised there, but you would be fortunate to meet more than one or two in a lifetime. If not in deep denial (and there are many who are, in subdivisions upon subdivisions, carved out of the bleak exurban desert), these hardy souls are engaged in the daily effort of home-building. Unsurprisingly, a good number of them are artists. Their art has no identifiable slant, however; few and far between are the earnestly pathetic at- tempts at communicating the trauma of finding a place amidst all that sunlight and lucre. But what they do all share is breadth, an individualism born of light, space and time. New York may be fertile, but LA is free.

In their art, the home shows up as it does in the rest of culture: nostalgically, or as an assertion of identity, or simply as an empty symbol, ready to be filled with whatever a viewer wishes to bring to it. The latter, while seemingly the most democratic tack, is usually the least interesting – both because we enjoy being voyeuristically entertained by the specifics of others' home lives, and because we want to be assured that our own are normal, either through identification or contrast.

However, most often, nowadays, the home appears in art as a lost object. This is significant when combined with the ob- servation that, increasingly, art no longer plays the role of the avant-garde – literally, where culture is heading – so much as it represents what culture has dropped along the way, or is in the act of neglecting: the places, marginalised or otherwise, where culture just will not go. Since art is going home, in fits and starts, obliquely as is its wont, it seems to me we should be paying attention – if only to see what we are missing.

Some have explained this loss of a sense of rooted place as due to a generation being raised amid modernism's smooth edges and space-age materials, and their attendant social fictions. But art and material culture do not act on history; rather, it's the other way round. More likely the phenomenon is the result of an alienation from history's rough-and-tumble: in this country, there now matures a generation of adults incapa- ble of remembering the last time friends and relations died fighting a battle that all agreed was just – or at least just adequate to threaten the obliteration of one's home, via arms or divisive passion. Plagues and inequities abound, surely, and causes have been championed, bureaucratised, ribbon- bedecked. But there is still a hollow at the core, a void that academe and politics cannot fill. In this era of detached affairs of state, of insulation bred of adequate defence, nutrition and education, the sense of home in our Western (art) world is less threatened than undervalued.

If artists are good for anything (and surely they must be good for something), they will let us know all of this, in their roundabout way. They will remind us that we are all snobs, believing we have no use for the trappings of home – that is, until we realise something is missing and then join those poor saps who spend their lives trying to plug the gap. Of course, I am speaking to a very specific audience here (you know who you are), one with room for art and theory and the luxury of introspection. And more decadently, with the time to listen. So, then. Welcome home.

New York, June 1996